NIGHT AND DAY

NIGHT AND DAY

A Play by
Tom Stoppard

GROVE PRESS, INC. • **NEW YORK**

822.9
St7nd

NIGHT AND DAY

Night and Day was first performed at the Phoenix Theatre, London, on November 8, 1978, with the following cast:

GEORGE GUTHRIE	William Marlowe
RUTH CARSON	Diana Rigg
ALASTAIR CARSON	John Bentley/Andrew Parris
DICK WAGNER	John Thaw
JACOB MILNE	Peter Machin
GEOFFREY CARSON	David Langton
PRESIDENT MAGEEBA	Olu Jacobs
FRANCIS	George Harris

The production was directed by Peter Wood and designed by Carl Toms, with lighting by Robert Ornbo.

Notes on Characters

GUTHRIE is in his forties, perhaps quite short, fit, can look after himself; wears tough clothes, blue denim, comfortable boots.

RUTH is in her late thirties, probably tall; attractive in face, figure and, especially, voice.

ALASTAIR is eight, English prep school; fair.

WAGNER is in his forties, a suit-and-tie man; big but not fat; an Australian; some accent.

MILNE is twenty-two or -three and definitely attractive in a way that is called boyish; casually dressed.

CARSON, Ruth's husband, is somewhat older than she is but also in good shape; casually but well dressed.

MAGEEBA, the President, is around fifty, a British-educated black African, a hard man if soft of voice; carefully dressed in freshly laundered "informal" army uniform.

FRANCIS, Carson's black African servant and driver, is in his twenties; slacks and white clean short-sleeved shirt.

A note on "Ruth."

The audience is occasionally made privy to Ruth's thoughts, and to hers alone. When Ruth's thoughts are audible she is simply called "RUTH" in quotes, and treated as a separate character. Thus, RUTH can be interrupted by "RUTH."

This rule is also loosely applied to the first scene of Act Two, where the situation is somewhat different.

The Set

An empty stage with a cyclorama, representing the open air, and a living room share the stage in various proportions, including total occupancy by the one or the other. Thus, the living room is mobile. The play begins with the empty stage (possibly a low skyline in front of the cyclorama). The room makes its first appearance by occupying about half the stage, the rest of the stage becoming garden. The first act ends with a reverse transition to the empty stage. The second act presents the room in its position of total occupancy of the stage. There is, however, a limiting factor: we have to have a good view of the interior of an adjoining room, an office-study, which contains a telex machine. We see the machine through the door of the study, when the door is open; and the door can also shut it out of our view. When we first encounter the living room, the study door being open, we can see that the telex machine is operating, that is, the paper is stuttering out of the machine. After Alastair's entrance our view of the machine does not have to be so direct. But, again, when the room is in its Act Two position we need a clear view of a man sitting at the telex. The telex is like a large modern typewriter, on a desk. It has to be "practical" and operate on cue.

We are in a fictitious African country, formerly a British Colony. The living room is part of a large and expensive house. The furniture is European with local color. It looks comfortable and well used. Essentials include a telephone, marble-topped table or sideboard with bottles and glasses on it, and a large sofa. The room should seat five people comfortably. The room could be connected with the rest of the house through a door, more likely double doors, or it might continue out of sight into the wings.

The first act—after GUTHRIE's dream—starts just before sunset, the last rays illuminating the garden; twilight follows quickly on this, and darkness has overtaken the play by the time of RUTH's second entrance.

ACT ONE

African sunset.

An open empty stage, the frame perhaps broken by the branch of a tree. There may be a low skyline. The cyclorama looks very beautiful. The sun is nearly down. The sky goes through rapid changes toward darkness.

A distant helicopter is heard approaching. By the time it reaches "overhead," darkness has fallen and there is moonlight.

Helicopter very loud. Shadow of blades whirling on the floor of the stage. Violent shaking of foliage. A spotlight from the helicopter traverses the stage. It disappears. A jeep drives onto the stage with its headlights on. Not much can be seen in the darkness. Two or three people in the jeep. GUTHRIE *is one of the passengers. The jeep turns toward the audience so one can only see headlights.*

By the time the jeep appears, a machine gun has started up. The noise is all very loud—helicopter and machine gun. The jeep probably isn't audible. The jeep hasn't stopped moving. The spotlight comes back and sweeps across the jeep. GUTHRIE *jumps out of the jeep and runs. He doesn't leave the stage. He just runs out of the light. The light loses the jeep. The jeep goes.* GUTHRIE *is shout-*

ing but it is hard to catch. He is shouting "Press! Press! You stupid fuckers!" Then the spotlight finds him. He stands up into the light with his arms spread out, shouting. The gun is firing bursts. He moves away from the corner. A burst catches him and knocks him over.

A late afternoon light reveals GUTHRIE *stretched out on a long garden chair. Sundown. The garden, with verandah/room beyond. The telex is visible and chattering in bursts like the machine gun; it is apparent that the noise of the telex had entered* GUTHRIE'S *dream in the form of machine gun fire. This noise has continued right through the transition of the scene. African rock music is heard from a cassette player placed on the verandah. This sound is joined by the sound of an approaching car. The telex stops.*

Not far from GUTHRIE'S *chair is his camera bag, with pockets for cameras, lenses, exposed and unexposed film, and other small objects. An empty glass is lying near the chair.* GUTHRIE *is apparently asleep.* FRANCIS *enters and removes the empty glass and exits again. The car arrives. The car door slams.* RUTH *comes into the garden carrying two or three packages which she puts down.*

RUTH: Those drums, those damned drums! (*She switches off the cassette player.*)

She sees GUTHRIE *on the chair in the garden.* FRANCIS *enters.*

RUTH: Francis, there's a man under that tree.

FRANCIS: Yes, ma'am. (*He exits.*)

RUTH *comes down and looks at* GUTHRIE *curiously.* GUTHRIE *doesn't move.* RUTH *notices the bag and bends down and touches it, perhaps to peer inside it.*

GUTHRIE: Please don't touch that.

RUTH: I'm sorry.

GUTHRIE: Christ. That wasn't nice at all.

RUTH: I thought you were asleep.

GUTHRIE: I thought I was dead.

FRANCIS *enters with a tea tray, a nice tea set with one cup and saucer.*

RUTH: Thank you, Francis. Has the garden been opened to the public?

FRANCIS: What's that, Mrs. Carson?

This gets through to GUTHRIE.

GUTHRIE: Oh—God—I'm terribly sorry—

RUTH: I shouldn't get up; you look awful. (*To* FRANCIS, *who is exiting*) Another cup.

RUTH's *manner is easygoing.* GUTHRIE *gets up.*

GUTHRIE: No—I'm fine. Sleeping on planes, you know. Ruins the complexion. From the inside. (*He has come up the steps toward her.*)

My name's Guthrie—George Guthrie.

RUTH: How do you do? I'm Ruth Carson. Would you care for some tea?

GUTHRIE: Wouldn't say no. Thanks.

RUTH *is pouring tea for* GUTHRIE *into the only cup.*

RUTH: Sugar?

GUTHRIE: No thanks.

GUTHRIE *goes back to his bag and fishes about in it. Meanwhile* FRANCIS *enters with another cup.* GUTHRIE *is looking for something—saccharin tablets—in his bag.* FRANCIS *exits.*

RUTH: I'm sorry I wasn't here to greet you Mr. . . . Guthrie. I had to go into Jeddu to pick up some things.

GUTHRIE: The boy let me in. I've come to meet Dick Wagner. (*English pronunciation—Wag-ner.*)

GUTHRIE *has found the saccharin and is coming back to the table.* RUTH *remains perfectly still. He gets to the table and sits down.* RUTH *waits until he looks at her.*

RUTH: What are you talking about, Mr. Guthrie?

GUTHRIE: Dick Wagner. Do you know him?

Pause.

RUTH: Is he a composer?

GUTHRIE: No. He's a reporter. Writes for the *Sunday Globe*, in London. I take the pictures. The pictures, as you know, are worth a thousand words. In the case of Wagner, two thousand. He was supposed to be at K.C. to meet me.

RUTH: Why in God's name do you expect to meet him at my house?

GUTHRIE: He told me. He left a message at the airport.

RUTH: He told you to meet him *at my house?*

GUTHRIE, *sipping tea, catches her tone for the first time, and hesitates.*

GUTHRIE: Well, he didn't mention *you.*

"RUTH": Help!

GUTHRIE: Just the house. The boy said it was O.K. to wait in the garden till Wagner comes. Is that all right?

"RUTH": "Is that all right?" Oh yes, bloody marvelous. Just what you needed, Ruth, and serve you right— nothing is for free, you always pay, and Guthrie has brought the bill. Silly woman!

GUTHRIE: Mrs. Carson?

"RUTH": Oh God, get me out of this before Guthrie's friend arrives; I don't feel up to being witty today.

GUTHRIE: Penny for your thoughts?

RUTH: Sorry?

GUTHRIE: You were miles away.

RUTH: Alas, no.

GUTHRIE: Sorry?

Pause.

RUTH: What kind of camera do you use?

GUTHRIE: Do you know anything about cameras?

RUTH: No. (*Pause.*) By the way, we don't call them "boy" anymore. The idea is, if we don't call them "boy" they won't chop us with their machetes. (*Brief smile.*) Small point.

GUTHRIE *holds his arm out, palm to the ground.*

GUTHRIE: Boy about this high, fair hair, your mouth, knows about cameras, has a Kodak himself; said I could wait in the garden.

RUTH *acknowledges her mistake, but* GUTHRIE *pushes it.*

His name's Alastair.

He has pushed it too far and she snaps at him.

RUTH: I know his bloody name.

GUTHRIE (*offering an olive branch*): The one I use mainly is a motorized F2 Nikon. (*Sips tea.*) Lovely.

RUTH (*smiles*): Would you like a proper drink?

GUTHRIE (*relaxes; shakes his head*): The sambo gave me a lime squash. (*Winces.*) Sorry.

RUTH *gets up; moves.*

RUTH: Why is my husband filling my house with journalists?

GUTHRIE: I thought he was one.

RUTH: Geoffrey? Don't be silly.

GUTHRIE: I saw the telex.

RUTH: That's for his business. Did he ask this man to come here?

GUTHRIE: I don't know.

RUTH: What does he want?

GUTHRIE: I don't know.

"RUTH": Help! (*Piano chords.*)

GUTHRIE: A story maybe.

"RUTH": I need somebody—help—(*Piano chord. It's the Beatles' song, "Help!"*)

GUTHRIE: What is his business?

"RUTH" (*picking up the rhythm*): Not just anybody— He-e-e-lp!

Car approaching.

GUTHRIE: Somebody coming.

He stands up and moves back into the garden looking out. Piano stops.

RUTH *laughs briefly at herself.*

GUTHRIE (*reporting from the garden*): Beat-up Mercedes. Is that your husband?

RUTH: It's a taxi.

GUTHRIE: Wagner.

RUTH *goes into the house.*

Helicopter approaching fast and low. GUTHRIE, *in the garden, looks up surprised. He sees the helicopter apparently coming straight at him. He cowers and goes into a crouch, his hands over his head. Shadow whips across the garden. Then the helicopter has gone. And we—and* GUTHRIE—*are now in the living room of the house. He is crouched over his bag, taking pills from it.*

ALASTAIR *has entered. He sees* GUTHRIE *crouched.*

ALASTAIR: What's the matter? Mr. Guthrie?   ,

GUTHRIE: Hello . . .

He swallows a pill from the pill bottle.

ALASTAIR *is carrying an old-fashioned leatherbound Kodak. The camera is folded and* ALASTAIR *holds it by the strap.*

GUTHRIE *straightens up.*

Hello.

ALASTAIR: I've found it. Are you going to show me about it?

Sound of taxi departing.

GUTHRIE: I think my friend has arrived.

FRANCIS *enters carrying the cassette player which is playing the tape as before.*

FRANCIS: I thought you were coming down to the compound with me, Allie.

ALASTAIR: No—I want to talk to Mr. Guthrie. (*To* GUTHRIE) I came before but you were asleep.

FRANCIS *exits.*

GUTHRIE: I'm sorry.

ALASTAIR: Will you show me later?

GUTHRIE: Sure.

ALASTAIR: I believe this is an excellent camera. It just needs some film.

GUTHRIE: When does your daddy get home usually?

ALASTAIR: That was him. The helicopter.

GUTHRIE: Oh.

Car drives away from the house.

ALASTAIR: He buzzes us. Then Francis takes the car down to the compound to fetch him.

GUTHRIE: The compound?

ALASTAIR: The mine. A helicopter is extremely useful in a country like Africa. Have you ever flown in one?

GUTHRIE: Yes, a few times.

ALASTAIR: In Africa?

GUTHRIE: No, in Asia.

ALASTAIR: Well, you know how useful they can be.

GUTHRIE: Yes. This is my friend, Dick Wagner.

WAGNER *has entered.*

WAGNER (*enthusiastically*): Hello, Gigi, you lovely bastard!

WAGNER *moves down into the room and slaps* GUTHRIE's *shoulder.*

You look *terrific!*

GUTHRIE: I look terrible.

WAGNER (*fresh start, same tone*): You look *terrible!* (*To* ALASTAIR) How are you?

GUTHRIE: This is Alastair Carson.

WAGNER (*talking down*): How do you do, Alastair? And how old are you?

ALASTAIR: Eight. How old are you?

WAGNER: Kid's a natural. This place is perfect for *Home and Garden.**

Female voice offstage, not RUTH, *"Allie!"*

ALASTAIR: Got to have my bath now anyway. (*To* GUTHRIE) Would you like to look at my camera 'til I get back?

GUTHRIE: Sure.

ALASTAIR: You won't forget.

GUTHRIE: No.

ALASTAIR: I'll come back.

Voice offstage: "Allie!" ALASTAIR *exits.*

GUTHRIE: How are things here, Dick?

WAGNER: Not wonderful. I've been in Jeddu for ten days. Bloody thing won't catch fire. Where's this Carson?

GUTHRIE: He's on his way. Who is he?

WAGNER: He runs the business end of the copper industry. Also manganese, potash . . . he's in mines generally.

GUTHRIE: But not frequently.

WAGNER: How about Mrs. Carson?

---

* Optional line referring to a large tree growing in the living room in the Phoenix Theatre production.

GUTHRIE: She keeps herself nice too.

WAGNER: Where is she?

GUTHRIE: Inside somewhere. Are you a friend of the family?

WAGNER: Hardly. The one who came out here was an earl or something. Grandfather, I think. There's an elder brother defending the title in England. This one works for a living. As it were. She's his second wife.

GUTHRIE: What are we doing here?

WAGNER: Looking up Carson.

GUTHRIE: Why?

WAGNER: I don't know. I think Hammaker must know him. (*He takes a folded cablegram out of his pocket.*) I got this on Sunday: "Guthrie arriving K.C. ex-Dacca Thursday. ETA ten hundred. Suggest uplook Geoffrey Carson at home Jeddu. Happy birthday. Hammaker." Did you tell her you were meeting me here?

GUTHRIE: Who? Oh, yeah.

WAGNER: You said me?

GUTHRIE: Yeah.

GUTHRIE *takes the cable out of his hand.*

WAGNER: Dick Wagner.

GUTHRIE: How many names have you got?

WAGNER: How did she react?

GUTHRIE: A bit like you.

WAGNER: How's Dacca?

GUTHRIE: You know Dacca. It's not Paris.

WAGNER (*nods; sings badly*): "April in Dacca . . . I love
Dacca in the springtime. I love Dacca in the . . ."
Yeah. It's not Paris. It's Dacca.

GUTHRIE (*handing back the cable*): Is it your birthday?

WAGNER: No. Sounds good, doesn't it?

GUTHRIE: Did you clock the telex?

WAGNER *looks around and sees the telex.*

WAGNER: Christ!

GUTHRIE (*nods*): Happy birthday.

WAGNER: I don't believe it.

GUTHRIE: Do you think he's got a wire machine somewhere?

WAGNER: We're going to make them sick.

GUTHRIE: Who's out here?

WAGNER: Everybody.

WAGNER *has gone to the machine. He taps a couple of
keys and waits for the evidence that it is in working
order. The machine chatters back at him briefly.*
WAGNER *looks at* GUTHRIE *wide-eyed.*

WAGNER: We are going to make them *ill.*

GUTHRIE: The hotel doesn't have telex?

WAGNER: The hotel doesn't have cleft sticks. There's a
post office in town which is a joke. Fritz Biedermeier
said when he blew the dust off the counter there was

an urgent message for Stanley from the *New York Herald*.

GUTHRIE: That wasn't here, was it?

WAGNER: It was a joke.

GUTHRIE: O.K. Who's Biedermeier?

WAGNER: *Newsweek*. He was in Beirut that time.

GUTHRIE: Oh yeah. Him. Has he got a photographer?

WAGNER: No, he's got a camera.

GUTHRIE: That's bad for trade.

WAGNER: Yeah, I wouldn't like it if you learned to write. I think we'll do O.K. now we've got wheels. Which is yours?

GUTHRIE: The Cortina. How did you get up from Kamba City then?

WAGNER: In a Cessna.

GUTHRIE: Bloody firemen.

WAGNER: Afraid of missing the war. It wasn't so expensive—I shared with a couple of photographers.

GUTHRIE (*interested*): Yeah?—who's that?

WAGNER: One was a Frog—Jean-Paul something. A Left Bank layabout. Yves St. Laurent army fatigues and a gold chain, very tough with the Gauloises, no filters—know what I mean? "I was just a gigolo till I discovered photo-journalism."

GUTHRIE (*sharply, angrily*): Knock it off will you, Dick? (*Pause; apologetically*) He's really very good.

WAGNER: Sorry.

GUTHRIE: What about the other one?

WAGNER: A groupie. No sweat. He had one of those cameras with a little picture of a cloud and a little picture of the sun and you slide it across according to the weather.

GUTHRIE (*smiles*): Well, I'm shooting Tri-X through two thousand quid's worth of lenses, but he'll get better pictures if he's in a better place. One time in Vietnam I was in a dugout with Larry Burrows, and this American kid is there—he looked like a hippie, bummed his way into the country and got himself a letter from AP and a secondhand Leica, so he's accredited, right?—wouldn't know his arse from a hole in the ground except he's *in* a hole in the ground, and he's lost his light meter. He's reading his Kodak packet, and there's all kinds of shit coming over, mortars, and he says to Larry, "Hey, do you think this is cloudy-bright or semi-dull?" Well, all you can see is smoke and flames so Larry says, "I think it must be cloudy-bright." This kid then starts walking forward behind a tank and the next time I see him he's got a set of prints of VC attacking the bridge, it looked like Robert Mitchum was just out of frame. Three pages in *Match.*

WAGNER: Maybe it's the same kid.

GUTHRIE: Later he stepped on a land mine.

WAGNER (*pause*): It probably isn't, then.

GUTHRIE: And Larry. And the other three in Larry's helicopter. Do you know how many people were killed in that war?

WAGNER: Not exactly.

GUTHRIE: Forty-five.

WAGNER: Oh. People.

GUTHRIE: And eighteen missing.

WAGNER: Don't be morbid, Gigi.

GUTHRIE: I'm not being morbid. (*Pause.*) Before you came I was sleeping, just out there, and I dreamed that I bought it—got killed by a helicopter. I was really quite spooked.

WAGNER: You were dreaming about Larry.

GUTHRIE: No—not in a helicopter *crash*—we were in a jeep and this gunship was shooting at us. And then it killed me.

WAGNER: For Christ's sake!

GUTHRIE: O.K. How are they getting their stuff out?

WAGNER: Air freight from K.C. There's nothing closer for pictures. Good chance of a pigeon, too—lots of people flying out at the moment. And there's the AP wire on Saturday if you're pushed—they'll print up for you.

GUTHRIE: Either way, it's a four-hour drive for that lot.

WAGNER: You won't do any better.

GUTHRIE: Carson's got a helicopter.

He sits down and picks up ALASTAIR's *camera and opens it. He's going to find a roll of film in his own bag and put it into* ALASTAIR's *camera. But this is something which he takes his time over, checking the camera itself, etc. Also, he gets interrupted so the job isn't completed until later.*

WAGNER: I can't take much more of this. Our own telex and a helicopter, and the competition writing post cards. If this war starts on a Saturday morning you and I are going to be famous.

GUTHRIE: You're famous in Dacca. I saw your name in the lavatory in the Inter-Continental.

WAGNER: How nice.

GUTHRIE: It said "Dick Wagner before he dicks you."

WAGNER (*grins*): Sour grapes. I didn't break any embargo. I had my own source.

GUTHRIE: All right.

WAGNER (*getting worked up*): By the time those stuck-up bastards woke up, my story was in London.

GUTHRIE: Listen, it's nothing to me.

WAGNER: Jesus—it was on the stone!

GUTHRIE: Do you think we're in the right place?

WAGNER: What do you mean?

GUTHRIE: I don't know what I mean.

WAGNER: Well, everybody else is here.

GUTHRIE: That's what I mean.

WAGNER: There's nothing better. Except an interview with the President, and nobody has even *seen* that mad bastard for six months.

GUTHRIE: What's the story in Jeddu?

WAGNER (*shrugs*): It's as near as we can get to ALF.

GUTHRIE: Who's he?

WAGNER: Them. "Who's he?" Don't you ever look at the bits between the photographs? A.L.F. Adoma Liberation Front. The Colonel. Colonel Shimbu.

GUTHRIE: O.K.

WAGNER: Didn't you know about my famous scoop?

GUTHRIE: No.

WAGNER: No, nor did I. Sunday, everyone gets cables from home. "*Sunday Globe* finds Colonel Shimbu. Why Shimbu unfound by you," etcetera. So everybody's screaming, "Where is Shimbu, Wagner, you bastard?" Only, it isn't my story. *I* don't know where the bloody Colonel is. So then they want to see my cable—they think it's a herogram from Hammaker. But of course I can't show it to them because I don't know what this happy birthday thing is all about. So then they're calling me a *lying* bastard, and following me to the lavatory when they aren't following armored car patrols into the bush in broken-down taxis. You never saw anything like it.

GUTHRIE: Yes, I did.

WAGNER: Yes, you did. There's a government press officer here who's the usual lying jerk, but there's no way of telling whether he's lying because he knows the truth or because he doesn't know anything, so you can't trust his mendacity either—he could be telling the truth half the time, by accident. His line was that the Adoma Liberation Front didn't exist, and the army had got it completely surrounded. But the *Sunday*

Globe knocked that one on the head. We heard it on the radio. The BBC World Service picks up this *Globe* exclusive and what do you know, George? Some sodding little stringer with no name has found Colonel Shimbu and made a monkey out of me. Yeah. It sounded like a good piece, too. I'd like to know how he got the story out. It was an interview with the Colonel himself. And furthermore, it's not a rebellion, it's a secession—get the picture? *Media credibility!* Well, the press officer goes bananas. He wants to know which side the *Globe* thinks it's on. So I tell him, "It's not on any side, stupid, it's an objective fact-gathering organization." And he says, "Yes, but is it objective-for or objective-against?" (*Pause.*) He may be stupid but he's not stupid.

GUTHRIE: I've got a present for you.

He gets up and walks toward the back of the room where he picks up a pile of newspapers. WAGNER *doesn't turn to see this.*

WAGNER: So he spends the briefing attacking the *Globe*— God bless him, it's the only story I've filed this week— and he's in a flat spin trying to make everything fit. At the end, this very smooth guy from Reuters says, "Let me see if I've got this right. It's not a *political* movement, it's just a lot—or rather *not* a lot—of completely illiterate ivory poachers who've been reading too much Marxist propaganda, and they're all armed with homemade weapons flown by Cuban pilots."

GUTHRIE (*coming back*): Who's the *Globe* special correspondent?

WAGNER: I don't know. I'm famous in Jeddu. Scooped by

my own paper. Bloody poaching, that's what it is. It's one of those ivory poachers moonlighting for Hammaker. I'd give anything for a copy of last Sunday's *Globe—*

GUTHRIE *dumps the newspapers into* WAGNER's *lap.*

Aw, Gigi!

GUTHRIE: I couldn't get them all, just what they had when I changed planes at Karachi.

The Sunday Globe *is a respectable English paper. The African story is the second most important story on the front page. The back page is a sports page. The other papers are: the* Sunday Express, Newsweek, *the* Sunday Times, *the* Sunday Mirror, *and the* News of the World.

WAGNER *of course looks at the* Globe *first.*

WAGNER: Second lead: "From a special correspondent"—

GUTHRIE: That's what I said.

WAGNER: What the hell does that mean? Fair old piece.

(*He turns the paper to look over the fold.*) Took care of mine anyway—"Richard Wagner adds from Jeddu" —two paragraphs. (*He puts the paper aside.*) Well, well. A world beat and no name on it.

GUTHRIE: A freelance.

WAGNER: They have names. I don't get it.

GUTHRIE (*picking up the* Globe): Where is this place?

WAGNER: It's sort of North Wales.

GUTHRIE: North Wales?

WAGNER: I've given up on place names here—they all sound like games you play on board ship. If a place isn't called Tombola it's called Housey-housey. The way to look at it is, K.C. is London, Jeddu is up the A40—Cheltenham—and the Colonel is somewhere in the Welsh hills. The *Sunday Times:* "At five minutes past eight on Wednesday morning, an aide-de-camp on the staff of Supreme Commander and President Ginku Mageeba, his uniform distinguished by Christian Dior sunglasses and unbuttoned flies, drove a green and white jeep up to the Princess Alice Bar in downtown Jeddu and commandeered it as the nerve center of Mageeba's victorious drive against the forces of darkness, otherwise known as the Adoma Liberation Front. The Army itself appeared in time for elevenses, and by today the advance had nearly reached the Esso pump three hundred yards up the road toward the enemy." Very funny. All facts and no news. (*He has found the inside page of the* Sunday Express *now, which reads:*) "The smoldering heart of this coffee-laden, copper-loaded corner of Africa is being ripped apart by the ambitions of a cashiered Colonel whose iron fist, UN observers fear, may turn out to be holding a hammer and sickle . . ." (*Scornfully*) And a New York date-line, who needs it? (*He tosses that aside.*)

GUTHRIE (*handing it over*): Newsweek.

WAGNER: Bloody Biedermeier. What's he got to say for himself? "This time last week Jeddu was a one-horse town on the road from Kamba City to nowhere. Today you can't see the town for cavalry, mainly armored personnel carriers and a few T-47 tanks. In them thar hills to the northwest, the renegade Colonel Shimbu is given no more chance than Colonel Custer —if only he'd make a stand. Unfortunately, no one can find the Colonel to tell him to stop playing the Indians and it may be that Jeddu is going to wake up one morning with its armored cars drawn up in a circle."

(*He throws that aside.*) I hate them and their Pulitzer Prizes. All writing and no facts.

GUTHRIE: *Mirror*—Nothing.

WAGNER: Well that's honest anyway. (News of the World —*he only glances at the front page.*) "Is this the laziest man in Britain?" I did that once. Different bloke, mind you.

WAGNER *turns his attention back to the* Globe, *which* GUTHRIE *has put down. He looks at it glumly.*

The dog barks. A car is arriving.

GUTHRIE: Carson.

WAGNER (*still preoccupied with the paper*): I don't think it's anybody who's been around much. It's good stuff but it's too much I-was-there. It's somebody who wants to impress the world and doesn't know that the world isn't impressed by reporters.

We have heard car doors.

Yeah, I think I've got this one's number—he's not a star, he's a boy scout in an Austin Reed safari suit who somehow got lucky.

MILNE *appears at the edge of the room.* WAGNER's *description is not far off.* WAGNER *hasn't seen him.*

(*Almost to himself*) Little prick.

MILNE: I say . . .

    GUTHRIE *and* WAGNER *look at him.*

    I say, that wouldn't be a *Sunday Globe*, would it?

    GUTHRIE *and* WAGNER *look at each other.*

WAGNER: Care to have a look?

MILNE: Not last Sunday's?! I say—*thanks* . . .

WAGNER: Have you just come with Mr. Carson?

MILNE: Yes, that's right. He's just gone up to see his wife.

    WAGNER *gives him the* Globe. MILNE *ignores the front page and thumbs through to the foreign page inside. His disappointment is silent but immense. He tries another page.*

MILNE (*miserably, scanning the paper*): He's just gone up to see his wife.

    WAGNER *and* GUTHRIE, *especially* WAGNER, *watch him like people watching a play, tensely waiting for* MILNE *to find his story.* MILNE *gives up and closes the paper, giving the front page a casual glance. Then he sees his story and the jolt he gets is audible.* WAGNER *and* GUTHRIE *relax.* MILNE *reads for a few seconds, lost in himself.*

MILNE (*to* WAGNER): Do you need this paper?

WAGNER: No. I'd like you to have it.

MILNE: Thanks awfully. (*Reading again.*) Carson's just gone up to see his wife and boy.

WAGNER: Yes, you said.

MILNE: Are you in mining as well?

WAGNER: As well as what?

MILNE *giggles and goes on reading.*

Anything interesting in the paper?

MILNE *finally puts the paper down.*

MILNE: Actually, I'm a journalist.

WAGNER: Oh.

MILNE: Actually, I'm on the *Sunday Globe.*

WAGNER: Ah.

MILNE: Well, I'm not actually *on* the *Sunday Globe.*

WAGNER: What are you doing here, actually?

MILNE: I'm covering the rebellion. This is my interview with Colonel Shimbu on the front page.

WAGNER: That's very good. How did you find him?

MILNE: A bit excitable but quite—

WAGNER (*hard edge*): How did you find him?

MILNE: Oh. It was a bit of luck really. Some of his men stopped a bus I was on.

WAGNER: What for? Food? Money?

MILNE: No. They give out leaflets and lecture the passengers for a while and let them carry on. But they took me off the bus. I was the only white. That was a month ago before the story broke properly. I was in

K.C. so I thought I'd have a recce, and I got kid-napped by this ALF group.

GUTHRIE: Lucky.

MILNE: Yes.

WAGNER: How did you get the story out?

MILNE: Shimbu got it out for me.

WAGNER: A pigeon?

MILNE (*laughing patronizingly*): A *pigeon?* No. We've got a little beyond that in Fleet Street. Shimbu gave it to one of his chaps to take over the border and he posted it for me.

WAGNER *glances at* GUTHRIE.

WAGNER (*expressionless*): Posted it.

MILNE: To tell you the truth the interview was ten days old but luckily I had Shimbu to myself. By the time the foreign press started to arrive in Kambawe the government got wise and attached the reporters to the army, which sounds promising but it takes away their freedom of movement. On a story like this it's no good at all until the real shooting starts. The story has got to be with the rebels. They should have known that.

GUTHRIE *smiles at* WAGNER.

WAGNER: Where was your last job?

MILNE: The *Grimsby Evening Messenger*.

WAGNER: The *Grimsby Evening Messenger*.

MILNE: That's an evening paper in Grimsby, in England. By the way, my name is Jacob Milne.

WAGNER: Dick Wagner.

MILNE: Hi.

GUTHRIE: Guthrie.

MILNE: Hello.

WAGNER: What are you doing here, Jacob?

MILNE: In this house?

WAGNER: In Africa.

MILNE: Oh. I lost my job in Grimsby.

WAGNER: Yes?

MILNE: My idea was to get myself in on a good foreign story without too much competition. Then I heard that there was this interesting situation developing in Kimbawe.

WAGNER: Where did you hear that?

MILNE: In Grimsby. (WAGNER *waits for more.*) I read it in *Time* Magazine.

WAGNER: Ah.

MILNE: Incredible how it's worked out. Carson says there's fifty reporters in Jeddu. They've got themselves thoroughly lumbered. There's no story in Jeddu. (*Reading from the* Globe) ". . . sources close to President Mageeba . . ." Sheer desperation . . . Richard Vahgner. I bet I've made him sick. Well, he's not going to be very pleased about my exclusive, and the awful thing is (*Looking* WAGNER *in the eye*) I've got another one. (*He sees the awful truth in* WAGNER's *eyes.*) Oh, Christ.

WAGNER: Sit down, Jacob.

MILNE: Look, I'm sorry—(*He turns to* GUTHRIE.) Are you with—?

GUTHRIE: George Guthrie.

MILNE: *Guthrie?*—Christ. I thought your Lebanon pictures were just—

WAGNER: Sit down. Where have you just come from?

MILNE: The Kaminco Complex—you know—I can never get these places right—what's it called?

GUTHRIE: Ping pong.

MILNE: No.

GUTHRIE: Deck tennis.

WAGNER: Shut up.

MILNE: Malakuangazi. About a hundred and fifty miles north.

GUTHRIE: What's Kaminco?

WAGNER: Kambawe Mining Corporation. Carson's outfit.

(*To* MILNE) How did you get *there?*

MILNE: With the ALF of course. Shimbu captured Malakuangazi this morning. He shelled it and then went in and killed the garrison. That's my story.

WAGNER (*stares at him*): Jesus wept.

CARSON *enters, heading for the study.* WAGNER's *interception is slightly ingratiating.*

Mr. Carson—I am Richard Wagner, *Sunday Globe.*

CARSON: Yes. Have you come to help Jake with his story?

WAGNER *decides to swallow that.*

WAGNER: That's right. My editor, Fred Hammaker, suggested I look you up. Sends his regards. And to Mrs. Carson.

CARSON: I'm afraid I've never heard of him. Excuse me.

Leaving WAGNER *looking at the closed study door.*

GUTHRIE: He's never heard of him.

WAGNER: I'm thinking about it. (*To* MILNE) How did Hammaker know about Carson?

MILNE: I told him.

GUTHRIE: When you sent your Colonel Shimbu piece.

MILNE: That's right. I thought Jeddu would be the next place I'd have a chance to file. I was right about that, though for the wrong reasons—like everybody else I thought the Colonel was heading this way.

WAGNER: You haven't filed yet?

MILNE: I couldn't. The land cable was cut in the shelling. That's why I came out in Carson's chopper. Do you know what Carson has got here?

WAGNER: Seen it. Happy birthday.

MILNE: I knew Geoff Carson slightly. I interviewed him for a background piece I did when I first arrived in the country. He wanted to check his quotes so he gave me his home telex number. I had it in my book. I told Hammaker it was one place he might be able to reach me.

WAGNER: And here you are.

MILNE: With bells on.

He takes his "copy" from his pocket and flourishes it. WAGNER *takes it from him.*

WAGNER: Well, you're a bloody idiot. You should have stayed inside and got Carson to carry your story out. He was the pigeon of a lifetime, with his own little helicopter. *Now* how are you going to get back in?

MILNE: Carson said he'd lend me a Kaminco car.

WAGNER: Don't be a clown—no one's going to get into Malakuangazi now without a tank.

GUTHRIE: Jacob?

MILNE: Yes?

GUTHRIE: Why did Shimbu let Carson leave?

MILNE: I don't know. (*Pause—apologetically*) I thought you meant a real pigeon . . . before. Sorry.

WAGNER (*to* GUTHRIE): What do you think?

GUTHRIE (*to* MILNE): Carson's using you for something.

MILNE: Does it matter?

GUTHRIE: Maybe not. I'll come with you.

MILNE: Fine. I never thought I'd be on a story with you.

GUTHRIE: Me neither.

GUTHRIE *relaxes, having settled his immediate future. He picks up* ALASTAIR's *camera and completes the business of inserting a film.*

MILNE: How interesting—I always imagined you'd have one of those flashy Japanese jobs with lenses and things . . .

GUTHRIE (*smiles*): There you go.

WAGNER (*with* MILNE's *story*): Is all this going to stand up? Twelve MiG-17s, three Ilyushin-28s—who told you?

MILNE: I watched them land this morning.

WAGNER: Where did they come from?

MILNE: Yemen. You can see why Shimbu went for Malakuangazi—I should have worked it out. It's not the mine, it's the airstrip. There's no strip at Jeddu for anything bigger than a Cessna. In the hills he had to make do with Mi-8 choppers to supply him from across the border.

WAGNER: Who flies them?

MILNE: Cubans. It's in there.

WAGNER: Did you actually see a Cuban flying a helicopter?

MILNE: Not exactly—

WAGNER (*flaring up*): Listen, Jacob—I know what it's like in Grimsby. You can say that Cubans have taken over the fishing fleet and next day you say that they haven't, *actually*, and nobody gives a bugger, because it's Grimsby. But this is the *Sunday Globe* and if you say Shimbu's got Cuban pilots you've got to have something better than his word and a Havana cigar—so who says they're Cuban?

MILNE: They do.

WAGNER (*pause*): You interviewed them?

MILNE: Not exactly interviewed—they wouldn't let me. We played cards a few times. I was just improving my Spanish. (*His irritation gets the better of him.*) And if you don't mind my saying so, Mr. Wagner, you know fuck all about the *Grimsby Evening Messenger*, which is a great deal more important around Grimsby than the *Sunday Globe* is around the globe on any bloody day of the week!

WAGNER: Please call me Dick. This guy with the field battery—did you talk to *him?*

WAGNER *is referring to* MILNE'*s pages.*

MILNE: Yes.

WAGNER: He spoke English?

MILNE: No, but I know a little Russian—it was my optional language at school.

WAGNER (*exasperated*): Tell me something, Jacob—what did you get fired *for?*

MILNE: I didn't exactly get fired. It was after the trouble in the provinces—you know, the strike.

WAGNER: Strike?

MILNE: The provincial reporters' strike.

WAGNER: I don't understand. You got fired for going on strike.

MILNE (*laughs*): Are you kidding?

WAGNER (*pause*): Oh no.

MILNE: Yes. It all seems a bit silly out here doesn't it?

WAGNER: Milne. You're one of those blokes all the fuss was about in . . .

MILNE: Grimsby.

WAGNER (*to* GUTHRIE): Do you see who we've got here?— It is the Grimsby scab.

MILNE: I say, that's not very nice.

WAGNER: Is it not?

MILNE: No. I don't keep an abusive vocabulary ready for anyone who acts on different principles.

WAGNER: Oh, acting on principle were you?

MILNE: Yes I was, as a matter of fact.

WAGNER: Is it your principle to betray your fellow workers when they're in confrontation with management?

MILNE *can't believe this. He almost laughs.*

MILNE: Come again?

WAGNER (*furious*): Don't patronize *me*, you little berk.

MILNE: I'm sorry—I was just taken aback. I never got used to the way the house Trots fell into the jargon back in Grimsby—I mean, on any other subject, like the death of the novel, or the sex life of the editor's secretary, they spoke ordinary English, but as soon as they started trying to get me to join the strike it was as if their brains had been taken out and replaced by one of those little golf ball things you get in electric typewriters . . . "Betrayal" . . . "Confrontation" . . . "Management" . . . My God, you'd need a more supple language than that to describe an argument between two amoebas.

But WAGNER *has already turned away to* GUTHRIE—*well worked up.*

WAGNER: "Special Correspondent!" That's why Hammaker never gave him a by-line! He knew Derek would never have worn it for a minute!

GUTHRIE: What Derek?

WAGNER: Battersby—Derek Battersby—Branch Secretary.

GUTHRIE: Battersby?—I went on something with him once . . . bloody useless reporter.

WAGNER: He's bloody good at squeezing the management. They don't always go together.

GUTHRIE: Do they *ever* go together?

MILNE: I thought foreign correspondents would find the whole thing a bit parochial.

WAGNER (*acidly*): I am not a foreign correspondent. A foreign correspondent is someone who lives in foreign parts and corresponds, usually in the form of essays containing no new facts. I am a fireman. I go to fires. Swindon or Kambawe—they're both out-of-town stories and I cover them the same way. I don't file prose. I file facts. So don't imagine for a moment you've stumbled across a fellow member of the Traveller's Club. To me you're the Grimsby scab. Jacob Milne. Yeah. What happened to the others?

MILNE: What do you mean?

WAGNER: It wasn't just you was it? Knocking out the paper like bob-a-job week?

MILNE: No.

WAGNER: Well I hope they're all making out as stringers up the Limpopo.

MILNE: They're all still on the *Messenger*. After the strike was settled the union expelled us, but the others appealed and got fined. Of course, the union didn't really want to expel me, they expected me to appeal too.

WAGNER: Why didn't you?

MILNE: I was feeling a bit wicked. The *Messenger* isn't officially a closed shop, you see—they'd just got used to having a hundred percent membership. I gave them a problem.

WAGNER: Smartyboots.

MILNE: I'm afraid so. But it backfired. By a majority decision they refused to work with me, and it looked as if the paper was going to shut down again, this time because of me.

WAGNER: So the management dumped you. You had to learn the hard way, didn't you? Bosses are bosses, and that's what it's all about, kid.

MILNE: I resigned.

WAGNER: Oh yeah.

MILNE: They refused to sack me.

WAGNER: They just heaved a huge sigh of relief when you went.

MILNE: Possibly.

WAGNER: Well, I hope the experience radicalized you a little. We're working to keep richer men than us richer than us, and nothing's going to change that without worker solidarity.

MILNE: I bet they don't come much more solid than you.

WAGNER (*wide-eyed to* GUTHRIE): Did you hear what he just said to me?

MILNE: The *Globe* is losing a million a year, and nobody's getting rich on the *Grimsby Messenger* either. It's not a private coal mine sending somebody's son to Eton, it's a limited liability company publishing a reasonably honest and not particularly wonderful local paper in the last two-paper town of its size in the country that began the whole idea of the right to publish, and you'd close it down out of pique—

WAGNER: What are you burbling about?

MILNE: We were called out because the *printers* had got a new deal.

WAGNER (*high*): Well, there were printers getting more than journalists!

MILNE: Yes, I know, but you make it sound as if the natural order has been overthrown. Fish sing in the streets, rivers run uphill, and the printers are getting more than the journalists. Okay—you're worth more than a printer. But look at some of this—

With his hand, or perhaps his foot, MILNE *spreads the newspapers and the* News of the World *lies in front of him.*

"We find the vanishing vicar of Lover's Leap!" "Sally Smith is a tea lady in a Blackpool engineering works, but it was the way she filled those C-cups which got our cameraman all stirred up!" It's *crap*. And it's written by grown men earning maybe ten thousand a year. If I was a printer, I'd look at some of the stuff I'm given to print, and I'd ask myself what is supposed to be so special about the people who write it—is that radical enough for you, Dick?

The feeling is that WAGNER *might actually hit him. Before we can find out whether he would have or not, the study door opens and* CARSON *comes out, head bent over a sheet of telex papers in his hand. He comes out reading.*

CARSON: "Onpass Milne. Congratulations Shimbu interview worldwide interest. Hammaker."

He hands this to MILNE.

MILNE: Oh . . . thanks.

CARSON: Sorry I had to leave you so long.

CARSON *nods at* GUTHRIE.

GUTHRIE: George Guthrie.

CARSON: George. (*They shake hands.*) . . . and . . .

WAGNER: Dick Wagner.

CARSON: Good. Geoff is my name. Should we have a beer? Or would you prefer something stronger?

GUTHRIE: Beer is fine.

CARSON: Dick?

WAGNER: Thank you.

CARSON: Sure you wouldn't rather have a scotch?

WAGNER: Much rather. Thanks.

CARSON *looks again at* GUTHRIE.

GUTHRIE: No—beer is fine.

CARSON: Jake?

MILNE *seems to be still reading the telex.*

MILNE: Yes?

CARSON: Beer or scotch?

MILNE: Yes—fine.

CARSON (*giving up*): I'll go and tell Francis. (*To* MILNE) You can try London now if you like.

WAGNER: We're very grateful to you . . . Geoff . . . most grateful.

CARSON (*into housephone*): Francis—bring some beer and scotch. (*To* MILNE) By the way you've got the spare room.

MILNE: Thank you.

CARSON *exits.*

WAGNER: I want to use that thing.

MILNE: How do you get London anyway?

WAGNER: You may be wasting your time.

MILNE: Why?

GUTHRIE: You're kidding.

WAGNER: No, I'm an officer of the *Globe* chapel.

GUTHRIE: That doesn't make it your responsibility.

WAGNER: That's right. Let Hammaker fight it out with Battersby at branch level.

MILNE: What is this?

WAGNER (*by way of answer*): "Onpass Battersby. Must protest employment of special correspondent Milne, non-member ex-Grimsby." Nothing personal. Send the piece. I'm not stopping you.

MILNE: Thanks a lot.

GUTHRIE: You *are* kidding.

WAGNER: Watch me. (*He goes to the study door and then invites* MILNE.) Watch me?

MILNE *goes into the study with* WAGNER, *who shuts the door.* GUTHRIE *takes a camera out of the camera bag and hangs it around his neck.* CARSON *returns.*

CARSON: Ruth's just coming down.

GUTHRIE: Okay if I take a picture?

CARSON: What for?

GUTHRIE: I don't know. Can I?

CARSON: I suppose there's no harm.

GUTHRIE *gets ready to take pictures, and is taking them over the next few moments until* RUTH'S *entrance.*

GUTHRIE: How can you get back into that place? Mala—

CARSON: Malakuangazi?

GUTHRIE: Yes.

CARSON: There's no way you can get me back. I was lucky to get out.

GUTHRIE: I mean . . .

CARSON: Oh . . . How can *you* . . .

GUTHRIE: Me and Jake.

CARSON: Jake asked me to help him.

GUTHRIE: Can you?

CARSON: Mageeba will have got his armor up there. You can't just stroll through.

GUTHRIE: What then?

CARSON: We'll see.

GUTHRIE: Do you know Shimbu?

CARSON: Yes.

GUTHRIE: Why did he let you out of Mala—

CARSON: Malakuangazi.

GUTHRIE (*pause*): I wondered if you were some kind of . . . I don't mean messenger—

CARSON: Emissary.

GUTHRIE: Yes.

CARSON *doesn't reply.* GUTHRIE *takes pictures. The telephone rings.* GUTHRIE *had just finished but this gives him a different sort of picture to take and he takes some while* CARSON *is on the phone.*

CARSON (*into phone*): Well, tell him to use the scrambler. I'll await his call.

Behind CARSON, *on phone, and* GUTHRIE, WAGNER *comes out of the study, closing the door behind him just as* RUTH *enters from within the house. When they see each other they pause, looking at each other.* WAGNER *smiles.* CARSON *hangs up and turns and sees them.* FRANCIS *enters with a tray of drinks, beers and scotches.*

CARSON: Ah, darling—have you met?

RUTH: No, we haven't. Mr. Guthrie told me you were expected . . . (*offering her hand*) Mr. . . . Strauss . . . ? (*She takes a scotch off the tray.*) Thank you, Francis. (*Her manner is amused, relaxed.*)

WAGNER: Wagner.

RUTH: Wagner. Exactly. I knew it was Richard.

WAGNER: How nice to meet you, Mrs. Carson.

FRANCIS *is moving around and the drinks are being taken off his tray.* RUTH *and* WAGNER *move down through the room and end up downstage.*

CARSON: We're Geoff and Ruth to everyone around here. (*He takes a beer off the tray.*) Isn't that right, Francis?

FRANCIS: Yes sir, Mr. Carson.

WAGNER (*taking a scotch off the tray*): Ruth, then.

RUTH: And I'll call you Richard.

WAGNER: Most people call me Dick.

RUTH: I'm not terribly fond of Dick.

WAGNER: You could have fooled me.

Their position in the room has enabled him to say this evenly.

GUTHRIE (*to* FRANCIS *for* RUTH's *benefit*): Thank you, sir.

RUTH: Well, that's that settled. Why don't we sit down.

"RUTH": And fasten your seatbelts. Ruth is taking no more nonsense from the pride of Wagga-Wagga.

RUTH: Where's the other chap? The one who came with you?

CARSON: Jacob Milne.

WAGNER: He's in there trying to raise London. Do you know London, Ruth?

RUTH: Oh, rather. Good old London, eh? . . . The red buses scattering the pigeons in Trafalgar Square . . .

CARSON: Yes, indeed.

RUTH: Covent Garden porters with baskets of fruit and veg piled on their heads, threading their way among the flower girls and professors of linguistics. Flexing their native wit against the inimitable banter of the pearly kings . . .

CARSON: All gone now.

RUTH: . . . The good old London bobby keeping a fatherly eye on the children feeding the beefeaters outside Buckingham Palace . . .

CARSON: Oh, all right.

RUTH: . . . giving himself a glancing blow with his riot shield every time a tourist asks him the time.

She turns her wrist to look at her watch and staggers back from an imaginary blow to the forehead.

CARSON: Don't be a rotter. (*To* WAGNER) How is London really?

GUTHRIE: Don't ask him—he's a bloody colonial.

CARSON: So am I.

Deep pause. RUTH *is amused.* CARSON *is forgiving.* GUTHRIE *apologetic.* WAGNER *helps out.*

WAGNER: It's quite true about me. When I first arrived in London I thought Fleet Street was between the Strand and Trafalgar Square. I was working from a Monopoly board.

RUTH: We play Monopoly with Alastair.

CARSON: Do we?

RUTH: On Boxing Day. As far as I remember Fleet Street was yellow and rather cheap. Is that right, Dick?

WAGNER: Not necessarily. Leicester Square and Coventry Street were yellow. To be fair you'd never confuse Fleet Street with Soho on the ground, you never saw anything so sleazy—the whole place has given itself over to crude titillation and eye-catching junk.

RUTH: And how about Soho?

WAGNER (*simultaneously*): . . . Soho. You're a caution.

RUTH: Where are you from, George?

GUTHRIE: London Wall. In the City. Of course, it's all been knocked down now. Bloody shame.

CARSON: Yes, indeed.

GUTHRIE: You should see it now. Do you know St. Paul's?

RUTH: I've heard of it.

CARSON: Actually, Ruth was born in London.

GUTHRIE: Really? Well, you wouldn't know it now. When were you last there?

RUTH: Friday.

GUTHRIE (*pause*): I think I'll just sit and drink my beer.

CARSON (*to* RUTH): You're a rotter.

The telephone rings and he gets up to answer it. Again he does more listening than talking.

RUTH: I'm a rotter, George. I'm a frightful rotter. I was picking up Allie from prep school, his first term at Ascot Heath.

ALASTAIR *comes in wearing pajamas and dressing gown and slippers.*

Hello, darling, your mummy's a rotter. Have you come to say goodnight?

ALASTAIR (*outraged*): Goodnight? I haven't even had supper.

RUTH: Well, go and see Winnie, she'll have it ready.

ALASTAIR: I want to talk to Mr. Guthrie.

RUTH: Mr. Guthrie will come and see you, won't you, George?

GUTHRIE: Never fear.

ALASTAIR: Will you come and see me in my room?

GUTHRIE: Promise.

RUTH: So will I. Say goodnight to Mr. Wagner.

ALASTAIR: Goodnight.

WAGNER: Goodnight, Alastair.

ALASTAIR: You won't forget, George?

RUTH: Mr. Guthrie to you—hop it.

> ALASTAIR *goes.* GUTHRIE *makes himself comfortable.*

RUTH: Oh dear, he's taken rather a fancy to George. Next thing, he'll want to be a journalist when he grows up. What is a mother to do?

> CARSON *hangs up the phone.*

Should I tell him it'll send him blind, and risk psychological damage?

CARSON (*leaving the room*): Darling, these gentlemen may not be used to your sense of humor. (*Calling*) Allie!

RUTH: Well I'm going to *need* a sense of humor if Alastair's going to go around the house putting his foot in the doors and asking impertinent questions. Perhaps I'll get him a reporter doll for Christmas. Wind it up and it gets it wrong. (*She seems in high good humor.*) What does it say when you press its stomach? . . . Come on, Dick!

WAGNER: I name the guilty man.

RUTH (*laughs*): Very good.

CARSON *comes back.* RUTH *gets up to replenish her glass.*

Yes, that's a question which has loomed large in my life—who's the guilty man? Until Geoffrey of course. Geoffrey is entirely blameless.

CARSON: Steady on, Ruth.

WAGNER: Who is the guilty man this time, Geoff?

"RUTH": Don't get cheeky, Wagner—he's not stupid.

WAGNER: There's always a guilty man—

"RUTH": Wagner.

WAGNER: —isn't there. Who do I name?

"RUTH": For God's sake, Wagner, there *are* rules and you're not going to break them in *my* house, drinking *my* scotch.

WAGNER: Shimbu or Mageeba?

CARSON: Oh . . .

"RUTH": Nice one!

CARSON: Depends which paper you read, doesn't it?

RUTH *takes her drink and sits apart from the men.*

WAGNER: What did the President have to say?

CARSON: Are you interviewing me, Dick?

WAGNER: Is that all right?

CARSON: No, it isn't.

WAGNER: Off the record, then.

"RUTH": Tell him to bugger off.

WAGNER: No attribution.

"RUTH": I'll tell him. Elizabeth Taylor in Elephant Walk . . . (*shouts*) "Get out of this house! This is no longer Geoffrey Carson's bachelor quarters, I'm his beautiful bride from England, and I'm sick of all you hooligans playing bicycle polo in my sitting room!"

CARSON *realizes that* GUTHRIE *has fallen asleep holding his beer glass.* CARSON *goes over and gently takes the glass out of* GUTHRIE's *hands.* ALASTAIR *returns stage left.*

ALASTAIR: Mr. Guthrie—

CARSON (*to* ALASTAIR): Hop it! Ten minutes . . . (ALASTAIR *exits. To* WAGNER) George tells me he'd like to get into Malakuangazi.

WAGNER: We both would. (*He holds up empty glass.*)

CARSON: Yes, of course. (CARSON *refills* WAGNER's *glass.*) What about Jake?

WAGNER: Jake is a freelance. I'm the *Globe*'s man on this story.

CARSON: He did well.

WAGNER: Yes, he did well. He had some luck.

CARSON: Was that what it was?

WAGNER: O.K., but now it's up to me to go where I can get ahead of the competition. There'll be a lot of journalists with the same idea.

CARSON: They haven't got a hope. The army won't let them through.

WAGNER: Can you help?

CARSON: Yes. I can give you a car, a driver who speaks the lingo, and a pass signed by the President.

WAGNER: My God, what am I doing for you?

CARSON: Colonel Shimbu didn't let me go for old time's sake. I was taking a message. You'll be taking the reply.

WAGNER: You were taking a message from Shimbu?

CARSON: Yes.

WAGNER: To President Mageeba?

CARSON: I didn't say that.

WAGNER: What *are* you saying, then?

CARSON: Use your imagination.

WAGNER: Unprofessional. What *I* use has to check out.

CARSON: Take it or leave it: I'm flying down to K.C. I'll be back in the morning, early, with a letter and the pass.

WAGNER: Signed by Mageeba.

CARSON: That's it.

WAGNER: And the letter too? (*Pause.*) Just say yes— (*Pause.*) Has Shimbu offered a deal?

CARSON: Come on, Dick. Well, you can assume I wouldn't ask you if I thought there'd be a war going on.

WAGNER: Why a journalist?

CARSON: Who else would want to go? I was thinking of Jake.

WAGNER: No. How long is the drive?

CARSON: About five hours. Lunch in Malakuangazi.

WAGNER: Friday lunch. Twenty-four hours to get back here and file. That's nice going if the Colonel cooperates.

CARSON: It might be better if Jake went. Shimbu likes him.

WAGNER: Shimbu will like me. I'm very popular.

RUTH: I've always wanted to meet a popular journalist. I mean socially, I don't mean under one's bed or outside the law courts. One is not normally introduced to journalists. I mention that as a matter of circumstance, not as a piece of social etiquette. Though, of course, it is that, too.

CARSON: I *thought* you were being unnaturally silent.

WAGNER: You don't much care for the media, do you Ruth?

RUTH: The media. It sounds like a convention of spiritualists.

CARSON: Ruth has mixed feelings about reporters.

RUTH: No, I haven't. I despise them. Not foreign correspondents, of course—or the gardening notes. The ones in between. I'm sure you know what I mean.

WAGNER: You've met one or two have you?

RUTH: Under the bed, outside the law courts . . . But don't imagine that I despise them because of any injury done to *me*—on the contrary I looked jolly nice in

my divorce hat and being on the front page of four
morning newspapers did my reputation nothing but
good in my part of Highgate—"Hasn't she done well?"
And even the indignities with which the whole saga
began . . . well, there are worse things than being
pursued across Shropshire by the slavering minions of
a Philistine press lord; in fact, it brought Geoffrey and
me closer together. I loved him for the way he out-
drove them in his Jaguar, and it wasn't his fault at all
that the early morning tea in our hideaway hotel was
brought in by a Fleet Street harpie in a tweeny . . .
no, no, it isn't that. It isn't even—or anyway not entirely—the way it was written up, or rather snapped
together in that Lego-set language they have, so that
poor Geoffrey's wife, a notably hard-boiled zoologist
who happens to breed rare parakeets, and who uncau-
tiously admitted to a reporter that, yes she would like
Geoff to give me up, and yes, she would have him
back, was instantly dubbed Heartbreak Parrot
Woman in Plea for Earl's Brother. Earl's brother.
That's the bit. Of all the husbands who ran off with
somebody's wife that week, Geoffrey qualified because
he had a measly title and if the right three hundred
people went down on the Royal Yacht he'd be Duke
of Bognor. *Has anyone ever bothered to find out
whether anybody really cares?* The populace and the
popular press. What a grubby symbiosis it is. Which
came first? The rhinoceros or the rhinoceros bird?

WAGNER (*gets up*): Sex, money, and a title—and the par-
rots didn't harm it either. I remember you now. Just.
The beginning of the gossip-column war. Nick
Webster was allowed thirty thousand pounds a year

for tip-off money. Thought he was the scourge of privilege. Thought the paper was behind him. Don't you love it? If someone had convinced the paper that the A/B readership has got bored with sex, money, and titles and had gone over to astronomy, Nick would have found himself on the roof with a telescope.

The study door opens.

MILNE: Dick! I got a line.

WAGNER: Yeah—I agree with you. Newspapers have got more important things to do.

He exits to the study, closing the door behind him. CARSON *crosses to use the phone.*

CARSON: You're riding him a little hard, aren't you? What's the matter?

"RUTH" (*rapid*): Matter? Matter? What do you mean, matter? What could possibly be . . .

CARSON (*as he finishes dialing*): Nothing wrong, is there?

"RUTH" (*as before*): Wrong? How do you mean, wrong? Why should anything be—

CARSON (*waiting for phone to answer*): What's up?

"RUTH": *Up?*

CARSON (*into phone*): Carson. (*Pause; turns back to her.*) Eh, Ruth?

"RUTH": Actually, Geoffrey, yes. Matter, wrong, up.

CARSON (*into phone*): Well, tell him it's me. Tell him I've got a courier fixed up. A journalist.

"RUTH": Geoffrey, there's something I have to tell you.

CARSON (*into phone*): Well, who else would want to go?

"RUTH": Geoffrey, darling, when I was in London I did something rather silly.

CARSON (*into phone*): All right—I'll be here.

He hangs up, but holds onto the phone, trailing its cord, coming back.

CARSON: If this thing comes off . . . (*He looks around vaguely.*) Where are they going to sit?

"RUTH": This is going to amuse you terribly, Geoffrey—

CARSON: Aren't you talking to me, Ruth?

RUTH (*turning to him*): I'm sorry I'm a rotten wife.

CARSON: You're not a rotten wife. I've had one of those.

RUTH: At least she was good at *something*.

CARSON: Parrots.

RUTH (*unjoking*): Yes—parrots. That's something. Parrot woman. You respected her for that at least.

CARSON: What's the matter?

RUTH (*insisting*): You must have been impressed.

CARSON (*studies her warily for a moment; and handles it*): Well, if someone comes up to you at a party, bites your finger and says, "Who's a pretty boy, then?" it makes an impression.

He wins a grimace-smile, and encourages her.

Come on . . .

RUTH: That's the disadvantage of being carried off as a virgin; it was years before I discovered I was brighter than most of the people I met. I mean, I could run the mines, Geoffrey, if I knew anything about mining. You know what I mean?

CARSON: Well, you nearly got your chance.

RUTH: I know, I'm a pig; you could have been dead today and I can't take it as seriously as my trite sense of failure. Oh, damn. I had a bad moment in London. Cried buckets.

CARSON: Why, what happened?

RUTH: Allie didn't have Cash's name tapes.

CARSON (*pause*): What?

RUTH: He was supposed to have Cash's name tapes sewn into every bloody gym sock. He was the only one without. Matron said, "Didn't he write to you? . . . He was told to write home for Cash's name tapes."

CARSON: Well, why didn't he?

RUTH: Exactly. Buckets.

CARSON: Well . . . it's not exactly "The Winslow Boy."

RUTH: I bet the Winslow boy had Cash's name tapes at least.

A sniff, the nearest she gets to a tear; then climbing back . . .

I could tell by the way Matron looked me over she'd *read* about sundowners and wife-swapping in the White Highlands. But, then, I was never meant to go

over big with school matrons. I was meant to be one
of those women who halt the cutlery as they pass
through hotel dining rooms on the first night of the
holiday . . . tits-first to the table through the ack-ack
of teeny-weeny diamond engagement rings. (*Pause.*)
I'm in the wrong movie, I think. I should be in "Ruth
Carson." Speakeasy queen.

CARSON: I really don't know what you're talking about
half the time.

RUTH: And that's the half I do out loud.

CARSON (*confirmation*): There you are. (*Pause.*) Do you
want a change?

Pause. The phone rings.

CARSON: Sorry. (*Apologetically*) Got to save the country.
(*Into phone*) Carson . . .

CARSON *takes the phone back across the room away
from her, doing more listening than talking.*

CARSON (*into phone*): Yes, sir . . . That's right . . .

"RUTH": Yes, I wouldn't mind a change, actually,
Geoffrey darling. Just a thought, you know. I had this
cowardly idea—delusion, I mean—that I might change
everything in one go by the pointless confession of an
unimportant adultery.

CARSON (*into phone*): Fine.

RUTH *lights a cigarette.*

"RUTH": I forget the title. (*Pause; loudly*) I have brought
shame on the house of Carson! Yes! It's Dick! He took

advantage of me, Geoffrey! I fought it, my God how I fought it! But I couldn't help myself!

CARSON *listening at the phone, half turns with his free hand stretched out toward her, his fingers ready to receive a lit cigarette.*

Don't shoot, Geoffrey!

She puts her cigarette between his fingers.

(*Casually*) By the way, Geoffrey, I let Dick Wagner take me to bed in London, in the Royal Garden Hotel, view over Kensington High Street, chosen for its proximity to the Embassy, in the visa section of which I met him while he was fixing his papers.

CARSON (*into phone*): Midnight.

"RUTH": I was fixing Alastair's. "Going out to Kambawe?" "Actually, I live there." "How interesting. I'm going out for the *Sunday Globe*. I say, you couldn't spare the time for a chat, could you?—spot of lunch—dinner —drinks—nightcap—" and so on. And so on. I believe it's called de-briefing. Not half bad either, though not as good as he thinks.

CARSON: Very well, sir.

"RUTH": Next day I picked up Allie and flew home.

CARSON *hangs up the phone.*

CARSON: It's on.

"RUTH": I didn't blame Wagner at all, 'til he showed up here looking for a second helping.

CARSON: I'm taking Allie.

"RUTH": That man is not a gentleman. Thinks I hop into bed with strange men because I hopped into bed with a strange man. (*Pause.*)

CARSON: All right?

"RUTH": I'm sorry.

CARSON: Are you listening. Ruth?

RUTH: I'm sorry—

CARSON: I'm taking Allie with me.

RUTH: What?

CARSON: He can stay with the Krebs for a couple of days. I don't want him here.

RUTH: Is it on, then?

CARSON: It looks like it. You must go, too. I trust Megeeba less than I trust Shimbu, and I don't trust Shimbu.

RUTH: Do you want me to go with Allie?

CARSON: No. I don't.

RUTH *kisses him. Nothing too special.*

RUTH: Then I'll stay.

WAGNER, *reentering from the study, almost catches this.*

WAGNER: Sorry.

CARSON: All right.

WAGNER *would have retired, but now closes the study door and comes forward.*

CARSON: I'll go and see how Allie's getting on.

CARSON *exits.*

WAGNER: Is it safe to come in?

RUTH: Why not?

She goes to the bar, and pours the remainder of a bottle of J & B into a glass for herself. It makes a large double scotch.

WAGNER: I had the feeling I was bad news.

RUTH: Bad news! Whatever gave you that idea? I name this ship Titanic—(*She smashes the neck of the empty bottle on the marble shelf.*)

RUTH *drops the rest of the bottle into the bin at her feet.*

(*Into house phone*) Francis. We're out of scotch.

WAGNER: You seemed to find me agreeable enough in London.

RUTH: And you thought I might find you just as agreeable in Jeddu, eh? That's something I forgive. It's crass but I forgive it. And just in case finding-you-agreeable-enough is supposed to be Australian understatement for blowing the lid off my billabong, let me tell you something, Wagner—if I had fancied you *at all* when you chatted me up in the visa office, I would have run a mile. That's what we honorable ladies with decent husbands do—didn't you know that? Every now and again we meet a man who attracts us and we run a mile. I let you take me to dinner because there was no danger of going to bed with you. And then because there was no danger of going to bed with you a second time I went to bed with you. A lady, if surprised by melancholy, might go to bed with a chap, once; or a thousand times if consumed by passion. But twice, Wagner, *twice* . . . a lady might think she'd been taken for a tart.

Pause.

WAGNER: What is it about *me* that makes *you* think that I would desert the international camaraderie of the Princess Alice bar in downtown Jeddu, and drive *all this way* across the smoldering heart of this copper-loaded corner of Africa, just to find out if *you* were still putting yourself *about?* Eh? What is it *about* me that makes you think that I don't know the difference between a woman on her fifth drink in a hotel room three thousand miles from home, and a woman ordering a fresh bottle from the servant quarters under her own roof, even when it's the same woman? Did you think that the twin social handicaps of Australia and journalism left me so unprepared for your mystery that I got culture shock when you took your Knightsbridge knickers off? What is it about *you* that makes you think it's likely? All I can see is a fairly interesting woman with a very boring problem: you don't know what you're doing here, and the days go very slowly. But I didn't come here to brighten up your day. This is a cable I got from my editor. I didn't know what it meant, but it turned out to mean that if I got off my backside I would find a private telex four miles down the road from a post office which has only just given up tom-toms; and I can't see anything in this room as beautiful as that telex. I am in love with it. I would have come on my hands and knees. Because I'm known for doing two things well: I can usually find out what's going on in a place while I am in it, and I can usually find a way to get the story back to my office in time to catch the first edition. It's not so much to be proud about, and if I fail nothing happens—not to Kambawe, not to the paper—but such as it is it's my pride, and what I want to know is, what are *you* so proud of that you can look at your life and sneer at mine. I mean, what is the secret of your success?

Both still. Pause.

RUTH: If you're waiting for me to say "ouch," you're going to get cramp. I don't share with strangers. All you're saying is, "Who do you think you are?" Well, I don't have to be anybody. So far, the only points you've scored are for not knowing a Marks & Spencer knicker when you see it. And as for that, don't tell me it never crossed your mind you might get lucky again.

WAGNER: As you'll remember, it wasn't that good. If it reminded you you were in love with your husband, that's good news for the world.

RUTH: I'm not in love with anybody. I just like some people a great deal more than I like others, and I like Geoffrey a great deal more than I like you. Is that all right?

WAGNER: Yes, that's fine.

RUTH: Good. (*She gives back the cable.*) Happy birthday.

ALASTAIR *comes in dressed to travel.* FRANCIS *brings a new bottle of J & B.*

RUTH: Come to give me a kiss, Allie? Thank you, Francis.

ALASTAIR: No—I want my camera.

RUTH: Be quick then.

> RUTH *exits.* ALASTAIR *goes to where* GUTHRIE *is sleeping. He kneels down and whispers to him.* FRANCIS *puts the bottle on the tray and sweeps the broken glass from the other bottle into a dustpan, and then exits.*

ALASTAIR: Mr. Guthrie . . .

WAGNER: Don't wake him. Here's your camera.

ALASTAIR: He said he'd show me how it works.

WAGNER: He put a film in for you. (*He finds the camera where* GUTHRIE *had been sitting.*) Here you are.

ALASTAIR: Oh . . . gosh, thanks. It's my dad's old camera really.

WAGNER: I say, I thought you were going to bed.

ALASTAIR: Daddy's taking me to Kamba City.

WAGNER: Why's that?

ALASTAIR: I'm going to stay with Krebs. Do you know him?

WAGNER: No.

ALASTAIR: He lives in K.C. He's my friend.

WAGNER: Oh.

ALASTAIR: I bet you don't know who my dad is going to see. I'll give you a hundred guesses.

WAGNER: Father Christmas.

ALASTAIR: No.

WAGNER: Mohammed Ali.

ALASTAIR: Getting warmer.

WAGNER: President Mageeba.

ALASTAIR: He told you.

WAGNER: Do you know the President?

ALASTAIR: No, I'm too young. That's why daddy's sending me to K.C. He doesn't want me here when the President comes.

WAGNER (*pause*): When is the President coming here?

ALASTAIR: Tomorrow night. Don't tell daddy I know it's him—he just said it was somebody coming.

WAGNER: And who told you it was the President?

ALASTAIR: My mum.

Offstage RUTH *calls "Allie!"*

WAGNER: Don't worry, I won't tell him.

CARSON *enters, followed by* RUTH *who carries a small suitcase for* ALASTAIR *whom she escorts through the door.*

(*With camera.*) You have to guess how far it is—you turn this, you see—three feet—six feet—and that's infinity, which means as far as you can see.

CARSON: Come on, Allie, into the car. (*To* WAGNER, *as* ALLIE *goes*) Allie was going to visit a pal in K.C.—so I'm taking him now—

WAGNER: I see.

CARSON: Might as well. Two birds with one stone.

WAGNER: What a childhood, eh?

CARSON: Yes. He's quite used to helicopters.

WAGNER: Yes, he was saying. Well, I hope everything goes well for you.

CARSON: See you in the morning.

WAGNER: Thanks, Geoff.

CARSON *goes out.*

WAGNER *stands still, thinking, and listens to the sounds of farewell, the car doors slamming, the car leaving.* WAGNER *is tense, and then he gives an inarticulate cry of triumph and punches his fist through the air like a goal-scorer. He moves quickly to* GUTHRIE *and slaps his hands together by* GUTHRIE's *ear, calls his name, and wakes him unceremoniously.* GUTHRIE *comes awake and stands up in the same moment, talking.*

WAGNER: Gigi!

GUTHRIE: I'm fine—I'm fine—where are we going?

WAGNER (*high as a kite*): I'm going back to the hotel. Need the car.

GUTHRIE *relapses into the chair.*

Keys! Listen, you're going to Malakuangazi, you and Jake, in the morning.

GUTHRIE: I should bloody think so.

WAGNER: I've got you a car, a driver, and a pass, and I've arranged a cease-fire. The *Sunday Globe* never sleeps.

GUTHRIE (*bitterly*): I know.

WAGNER: I'll cover this end.

RUTH *returns to the room.*

RUTH: George—poor George—when did you last sleep in a bed?

GUTHRIE: I was just pretending to be asleep. It's an old photographer's trick.

RUTH: Oh yes, I'm sure.

GUTHRIE: I promised to go and see Alastair—

RUTH: Oh dear—you've missed him—

GUTHRIE: Missed him?

WAGNER: I gave him the camera. You'll see him next time. (*To* RUTH) I'm taking George to the hotel.

RUTH: There's room in the dorm. Geoffrey arranged it.

WAGNER: Well, that *would* be better. It's going to be quite an early start.

GUTHRIE: Yes, thanks. I'll get my stuff out of the car.

RUTH: We eat early.

GUTHRIE *goes out: "Fine, thanks."*

RUTH: I hope you don't mind sharing a room?

WAGNER: You're a sport, Mrs. Carson, but let's just be friends.

RUTH: Bastard.

WAGNER: I made an excuse and left.

WAGNER *is leaving but* MILNE *comes out of the study holding a piece of telex.* MILNE *doesn't see* RUTH.

MILNE: Dick, I've got your reply—

WAGNER: What?

MILNE (*slightly embarrassed*): The reply to your, um, protest . . .

WAGNER: Oh yes? From Battersby?

MILNE: From Hammaker.

WAGNER: Well, what does it say?

MILNE: "Onpass Wagner. Upstick protest arsewards."

WAGNER: This is Jacob Milne. He'll be making the trip with George. You're staying the night here, Jake, leaving early tomorrow. Geoffrey will fill you in.

MILNE: Fine.

WAGNER: If the land cable is still out, one of you'd better get back here to file early Saturday to be safe. Either give Gigi your copy or bring his film out.

MILNE: Okay. Don't worry.

WAGNER (*to* RUTH): Thanks, Ruth. For everything.

MILNE (*to* WAGNER): What will you do?

WAGNER: Best I can.

MILNE: No hard feelings?

WAGNER: It was your story anyway. (*He's going but a thought strikes him.*) Why did you choose the *Globe?*

MILNE: Well, Hammaker started on the *Grimsby Messenger.* Didn't you know that?

WAGNER: No, I didn't.

MILNE: Yes. He's famous in Grimsby.

WAGNER (*smiles*): I bet.

WAGNER *goes.* RUTH *sits down.*

RUTH: How do you do.

MILNE: How do you do.

RUTH: What was that about no hard feelings?

MILNE: Dick isn't very happy about the *Globe* using me. He's a strong union man.

RUTH: And you're not.

MILNE: It's not that. It's just that I think journalism is . . . special. Dick thinks I'm naive about newspapers.

RUTH: And you're not?

MILNE: I don't think so. Do you think I am?

RUTH: I haven't really had time to form an opinion.

MILNE: He thinks the *Globe* is a million packets of journalism manufactured every week by businessmen using journalists for their labor.

RUTH: That *is* what the *Globe* is.

MILNE: No, it's not. A free press, free expression—it's the last line of defense for all the other freedoms.

RUTH: I've formed an opinion.

MILNE (*laughs*): No, really—

RUTH: Why don't you sit down?

MILNE: No, thanks.

RUTH: Would you like a drink?

MILNE: No, thanks.

RUTH (*holding out her empty glass*): Would you be good enough . . . ?

MILNE (*taking the glass*): Of course.

RUTH *gets up.*

RUTH: Scotch.

"RUTH": Watch yourself, Tallulah.

The scene now moves into the garden.

MILNE (*doing the drink*): Dick wants union membership to be a license to practice. "This man has been judged fit."

He joins RUTH *and gives her the scotch. She goes further into the garden and* MILNE *follows her.*

Like doctors and lawyers, I suppose.

RUTH: Nothing wrong with that. Otherwise you'd have lawyers amputating the wrong leg. Ho, ho—

"RUTH": You're giggling. Shut up.

RUTH: Mining engineers have the same sort of thing, I believe. Professional standards.

MILNE: Oh, yes. But nothing could be further from Dick's mind. The fact is nobody's going to be drummed out of the NUJ for illiteracy or getting drunk at the Lord Mayor's dinner. On the contrary it's the union which is going to keep them in their jobs. No, what Dick wants is a *right-thinking press*—one that thinks like him.

RUTH: So what? You'd like a right-thinking press, too. One that thinks like you.

MILNE: Sure I would, but I don't intend to get it by blacklisting *him*.

RUTH: Perhaps you should.

MILNE: Think about it.

RUTH (*pause*): Yes, quite.

"RUTH": This party's looking up—who's this rather interesting young man?

MILNE: Once you establish the machinery it'll be there for someone else to use. Drum you out if you're too left-wing, or not left-wing enough, or the wrong color, or something.

RUTH: Well, it would be up to you, wouldn't it? Everybody's got a vote.

MILNE: Everybody who's allowed in would have a vote, yes.

RUTH: You're an alarmist, Jacob. On the whole people behave responsibly.

MILNE: On the whole because their behavior is observed. Reported.

RUTH: You're a cynic.

MILNE: Me?

RUTH: No, that can't be right.

MILNE: It wouldn't be like the Law Society or the BMA.

RUTH: It would in principle. If *any* group got control of

the Law Society, they'd be just as free to have only right-thinking solicitors. What then?

MILNE: Then you'd *really* need a free press, otherwise you may never find out about it. That's the whole point. No matter how imperfect things are, if you've got a free press everything is correctable, and without it everything is concealable.

RUTH: I'm with you on the free press. It's the newspapers I can't stand.

MILNE: You don't have to tell me, I know it better than you—the celebration of inanity, and the way real tragedy is paraphrased into an inflationary spiral of hackneyed melodramas—Beauty Queen In Tug-of-Love Baby Storm . . . Tug-of-Love Baby Mum In Pools Win . . . Pools Man In Beauty Queen Drug Quiz. I *know*. It's the price you pay for the part that matters.

"RUTH": I like that one who's doing all the talking.

MILNE: It's not easy to defend, but it's mainly attacked for the wrong reasons. People think that rubbish journalism is produced by men of discrimination who are vaguely ashamed of truckling to the lowest taste. But it's not. It's produced by people doing their best work. Proud of their expertise with a limited number of cheap devices to put a shine on the shit. Sorry. I know what I'm talking about because I started off like that, admiring it, trying to be *that good*, looking up to Fleet Street stringers, London men sometimes, on big local stories. I thought it was great. Some of the best times in my life have been spent sitting in a clapped-out Ford Consul outside a suburban house with a packet

of Polos and twenty Players waiting to grab a crooked
landlord or a footballer's runaway wife who might be
good for one front page between oblivion and oblivion. I felt part of a privileged group, inside society
and yet outside it, with a license to scourge it and a
duty to defend it, night and day, the street of adven-
ture, the fourth estate. And the thing is—I was dead
right. That's what it was, and I *was* part of it because
it's indivisible. Junk journalism is the evidence of a society that has got at least one thing right, that there
should be nobody with the power to dictate where responsible journalism begins. (*Pause.*) I'm not usually
so wound up. It's been an amazing day. I was the only
reporter in Malakuangazi, you know. I mean, that
story I sent over, it's probably the best story I'll ever
get in my life.

RUTH: You must be tired.

MILNE: Not a bit.

RUTH: Hungry?

MILNE: Starving.

RUTH: Then let's eat.

MILNE: I'm sorry I talked so much.

RUTH: No. I like you to talk.

She looks at him steadily, too long for his comfort.

MILNE: Thanks very much for letting me stay. I'll go and
sort myself out.

MILNE *goes into the lighted house.* RUTH *stays in the
dark.*

"RUTH": Run. Run, you stupid bitch.

RUTH *exits.*

Night into day.

Dawn.

The jeep drives in. FRANCIS *at the wheel.* CARSON *comes out of the house, shortly followed by* GUTHRIE, GUTHRIE *has changed some of his clothes, still blue denim or something non-military. He has his camera bag and another shoulder bag.* CARSON *shouts up as though to an upstairs window.*

CARSON: Jake! Francis, I want this back in one piece. (*Pats jeep.*)

FRANCIS: Yes, sir.

CARSON: You, too, of course. Take it easy.

FRANCIS: Yes, sir, Mr. Carson.

CARSON (*turns and sees* GUTHRIE, *who has just entered*): All set? Where's Jake?

GUTHRIE: What's that?

CARSON: What's it look like?

GUTHRIE: It looks like a stunted* jeep. Wagner said a car.

CARSON: What's the difference? Car, jeep. This isn't a trip for a family saloon.

GUTHRIE *is very angry and upset but still controlled.*

GUTHRIE: A family saloon is neutral. That thing is a tar-

---

* e.g. Mini-Moke if Jeep is too large for stage.

get. Listen—I know the game. I know the edge on every hand I'm dealt. It was the same in the Congo, Angola, Somalia. And it's the same here.

Then he sees that MILNE *has come out of the house wearing army type clothing, including a camouflage-colored cotton bush hat.*

(*Explodes*) Oh, *bloody hell*, he's dressed up like Action Man!

GUTHRIE *takes the hat off* MILNE'S *head and throws it on the ground.*

MILNE: What's the matter? (*He picks up the hat.*)

GUTHRIE: You don't drive into an African war in a khaki shirt with epaulettes!

CARSON: What war? There isn't going to be any war today.

MILNE: I've got a tennis shirt in my bag—I'll change if you like.

GUTHRIE: Did you bring your racket?—*This is crazy.* Wagner should have done the trip.

MILNE: Thought you were on my side. Come on, Gigi—

He goes toward the jeep, and toward CARSON.

CARSON: Jake. Here's the letter. For God's sake don't lose it.

MILNE *puts the letter in his bag, then gets into the jeep.* FRANCIS *guns the engine a little.* GUTHRIE *stands looking at the ground.*

MILNE: Well, are you coming or not?

GUTHRIE (*looks at the ground; quietly*): Oh, shit.

Then he moves quickly to the jeep, puts his camera bag on board, and swings on behind as the jeep starts to move.

Blackout.

ACT TWO

The room at night.

The room occupies the whole stage now.

RUTH *sits in one of the comfortable chairs. She is wearing a long dress, not formal but loose and comfortable, perhaps a kaftan; more dressed up than we have seen her, rich material but not gaudy. She sits facing the audience.*

The room is not brightly lit, and the edges are in gloom.

MILNE *stands at the edge of the room.*

"RUTH": Hello, Jacob, I'm glad it's you. I've been holding my breath since I heard the jeep. I'm glad you're back. I missed you, Jake.

RUTH *sees him.*

RUTH: Oh—hello!

MILNE: Hello. Thought you were having a snooze.

RUTH: No, no. Good trip?

MILNE: Yes, thanks. Piece of cake.

RUTH: Lots of scoops?

MILNE: Masses.

RUTH: Come and sit down.

MILNE: Thank you.

RUTH: Have a drink.

MILNE: No thanks. Where's Geoffrey?

RUTH: He's away.

MILNE: I thought everybody would be asleep.

RUTH: I felt like waiting up. Are you all right?

MILNE: Never better.

RUTH *laughs*.

What's up?

RUTH: Nothing. I like the way you have such a good time. Dashing around for the glory of the *Globe*. Grimsby man in *Globe* glory dash.

MILNE: You do think I'm naive.

RUTH: No I don't.

MILNE: Too young and idealistic.

RUTH: That's different.

MILNE: I expect I'll end up like Dick.

RUTH: I hope not.

MILNE: Dick's all right. He's a bit . . .

RUTH: Wagnerian.

MILNE: I suppose he's gone off with the press corps.

RUTH: I suppose so. It's nice that you've got us to come back to.

MILNE: Yes—a line to London on tap—one couldn't ask for more. Oh—and present company included, of course.

"RUTH": Help.

MILNE: Well, I expect you'd like to go to bed.

"RUTH": I'm over here.

MILNE: I've got a piece to write.

"RUTH": To hell with that.

MILNE: You won't mind if I try to get London later?

"RUTH": And to hell with London.

MILNE: I'm sure Geoffrey wouldn't mind. Is he in K.C.?

"RUTH": Why don't you shut up and kiss me.

MILNE: He said I could help myself.

"RUTH": So kiss me.

MILNE: Perhaps I should try for a line first—let them know I'm here.

RUTH: I would prefer you to kiss me.

MILNE: Kiss you?

Pause. RUTH *blinks and turns to him.*

RUTH: Yes.

MILNE: Well . . . um, I was just saying, I ought to establish contact with the office.

RUTH: Yes. I think that would be a very sensible idea.

MILNE: Thank you.

RUTH: But isn't it rather late, or early, or something?

MILNE: It is here.

RUTH: Oh yes. We seem to have got off the subject.

MILNE: Have you been out this evening?

RUTH: No. Why?

MILNE: You look—a bit dressed up.

RUTH: This old thing? I just threw it on as I stepped out of the shower.

MILNE: Ah. Jolly nice.

RUTH: Wouldn't do for the Club at all.

MILNE: Is there a club?

RUTH: The Jeddu Country Club. Very quiet since independence. They used to have Coronation dances, I believe. Now it's billiards, bar, and smoking room. I don't play billiards but I drink and smoke. And they get all the important magazines—*Country Life, Mining Review, Kambawe Today* . . . and, you'll be interested to hear, some of the London papers.

MILNE: Doesn't sound bad at all. Are they flown in?

RUTH: I don't think so. We're still getting the *Morning Post*. It's all right, you don't have to kiss me at all.

MILNE: It isn't that I don't think you're attractive.

RUTH: No. It's just that Geoffrey has been damned decent to you . . .

MILNE: Well, yes. And even if he hadn't . . .

RUTH: It wouldn't be right to make free with his possessions—his ox, his ass, his wife—

MILNE: Wait a minute. (*He pauses, concentrating for
four or five seconds—he looks at her.*) No.

RUTH: Well, I'm glad it wasn't instantaneous.

MILNE: I mean your argument. It sounds good but it's
not. I *might* make free with his ox and his ass—or his
jeep—because they *are* merely his possessions. But if I
indulged my desire for you I would be numbering you
among them. As it is, it seems I regard a wife as
different from a jeep, which puts me in the forefront
of enlightened thinking. (*Smiles.*) Wouldn't you say?

RUTH: What desire for me?

MILNE: Oh, crikey.

RUTH: Had any lewd thoughts?

MILNE: I told you I found you attractive.

RUTH: Tell me about the lewd thoughts.

MILNE: No.

RUTH: Oh, come on. Don't be such a spoilsport. There
you are, in the jeep. The sun beats down. Tracker
Francis is keeping his eye on the road. Bwana Guthrie
is taking pictures of nature and poverty for the color
magazine. Your thoughts drift . . . "I say, that Ruth
Carson, she's all woman." Carry on from there.

MILNE *won't.*

Did you undress me?

MILNE: No.

RUTH: I kept my clothes on?

MILNE: You undressed yourself.

RUTH: Ah. Was it dark or daylight? On a bed? On the floor? Long grass? In the jeep? (*Pause.*) It was in the jeep.

MILNE (*sharply*): No, it wasn't. (*Pause.*) It was in a parallel world. No day or night, no responsibilities, no friction, almost no gravity.

RUTH: I know it. How was I?

MILNE (*exasperated*): *Ruth.*

RUTH: You were *good.* (*Pause.*) It's about *time* you called me Ruth.

MILNE: Show some, then. Ruth: that which is lacking in ruthlessness. It comes into Milton. "Look homeward angel, now, and melt with ruth." Compassion—contrition. Something like that.

RUTH: I'm not really a tart.

MILNE: No—of course.

RUTH: I was almost a tart with my first husband, but he was a rotter in his own way. He was frankly proud of his left hook.

MILNE: Was he?

RUTH: Unjustifiably so. You could slip it quite easily and get him with a right cross. What a way to live. To get *me,* all Geoffrey had to do was clear his throat and hold the door.

MILNE: Did you love him too?

RUTH: Of course I loved him—loved Africa. Just like Deborah Kerr in *King Solomon's Mines* before the tarantula got into her camiknickers. And I haven't been a tart with Geoffrey. Slipped once, but that was in a hotel room and hotel rooms shouldn't count as infidelity. They constitute a separate moral universe. Anyway, I had terrible PCR, and a tart wouldn't, would she?

MILNE: What's PCR?

RUTH: Post-coital remorse. Post-coital ruth. Quite needlessly—I mean, it's a bit metaphysical to feel guilt about the idea of Geoffrey being hurt if Geoffrey is in a blissful state of ignorance—don't you think?

MILNE: No.

RUTH: No. Fresh start. Hello!—had a good trip? (*Pause.*) I don't know. I got into a state today. I'm telling you this because it is very boring, you understand. Went to bed feeling nothing more dangerous than a heightened sense of you being in the house. Woke up fluttering with imminent risk. Quite a pleasant feeling, really. Like walking along the top board knowing you don't have to jump. But a desperate feeling, too, because if you're not going to jump what the hell are you doing up there? So I got dressed to say goodbye to you. Really. Dressed for it. "What shall I wear to say goodbye to Jake?" Don't feel flattered. You look like you look, and you've got a way of being gauche which suggests that you've got the edge on people who know the ground and prepare their effects—I was attracted, as it happens, but it's like throwing a pair when you've got three-of-a-kind on the table. This time, bingo, but no use at all to anyone looking for a straight. Anyway, while I was dressing for this intensely laconic fare-well, you'd been gone an hour. Geoffrey hadn't wanted to wake me. He's thoughtful about things like that. Saying goodbye would have taken care of it, I expect. It was finding you gone that did it. *Quietus interruptus.* I went peculiar. I lost my view of myself. I was unembarrassable. Your sheets were cold. Pillow had no smell.

Pause.

You say something.

MILNE: You were good, too. (*Pause.*) You shouldn't try to make it sound like a free ride. "Geoffrey will never know and I'm not his chattel so there's nothing to pay." There are no free rides. You always pay.

RUTH: Take it, then, and pay. Be a bastard. Behave badly.

MILNE: That's better.

RUTH: Betray your benefactor.

MILNE: That's right.

RUTH: Corrupt me.

MILNE: Put it like that, I might.

RUTH: Steal me.

MILNE: I want to.

RUTH: Good. Mess up my life. I'll pay.

MILNE: Stupid.

RUTH: Don't be frightened.

MILNE: And tomorrow—

RUTH: I'll pack if you like. If you don't like, I'll stay and deadhead the bougainvillaea. Either way I'll pay.

They kiss on the mouth, but not passionately and not holding each other.

MILNE: Leave me alone. You should know better.

RUTH: I do know better. To hell with that.

She lets herself fall over backwards onto the sofa. Only her calves and feet are visible.

(This may not be a practical idea: in the first production RUTH *went behind the tree which stood in the middle of the room, and her double came from behind the tree.)*

MILNE *turns and walks upstage into the dark.* RUTH'*s feet disappear out of sight behind the sofa and then she (her double) stands up with her back to the audience looking toward where* MILNE *disappeared. Then she undoes her dress and steps out of it (she has nothing on underneath), holding on to the dress with one hand and trailing it after her as she follows* MILNE *into the dark. Before she has disappeared* CARSON *has walked unhurriedly, relaxed, into the room from the study. He lights a cigarette and stands thoughtfully, watching as "*RUTH*" moves into the dark. After a moment or two,* RUTH *reappears where we last saw her.*

RUTH: Got a cigarette for me?

CARSON: There's no need for you to stay up.

RUTH: I want to.

CARSON: He may not come for hours.

RUTH: I'm all right. What time is it?

CARSON (*looks at his watch*): Saturday. Nearly one. You got dressed up for him.

RUTH: Well, he is the President.

The dog starts barking.

CARSON: Here we go.

CARSON *moves to a light switch and the exterior lights come on. Sound of an approaching vehicle.* CARSON *leaves the room.*

RUTH *moves to a chair. She puts out her cigarette.*

The vehicle has arrived. CARSON *opens the door—goes to meet the arrival.*

CARSON (*offstage*): Oh—God!

WAGNER (*entering*): Hello!

CARSON (*entering*): Any other time, old man—

WAGNER: I saw your lights from the road.

CARSON (*entering*): Ruth and I were just going to bed.

WAGNER (*to* RUTH): Good evening. I brought a nightcap. (*He's carrying a bottle of Cutty Sark whisky, not a full one.*) Compliments of the firm. I'm afraid I've started without you. (*He's making himself at home. He puts the bottle down.*) I saw the lights as I was passing.

RUTH: The lights weren't on as you were passing.

CARSON: Look, Dick, not this time, there's a good fellow.

WAGNER: Have a heart—all this way for a nightcap.

CARSON: You said you were passing—

WAGNER: To see if you were up.

CARSON: Well, we were just turning in, weren't we, darling? Why don't you drop in tomorrow—*today,* for heaven's sake—for a sundowner.

RUTH: Leave off, Geoffrey—he knows. (*To* WAGNER) You do know, don't you?

WAGNER: Oh, absolutely.

CARSON: Knows what?

RUTH: He knows we're waiting for Mageeba.

CARSON (*angrily*): Ruth . . .

WAGNER: Mageeba—that's the fellow.

CARSON: It's a social call.

WAGNER: Isn't it, though?

CARSON: He likes to eat late.

WAGNER: Yes, I heard. When is Colonel Shimbu coming?

CARSON: He's not coming.

RUTH (*simultaneously*): In the morning. (*Pause.*) He's not coming in the morning.

CARSON: This is dreadful.

WAGNER: I'll be as quiet as a mouse.

CARSON: Mageeba is going to be furious. You'll be lucky if you don't end up under arrest.

WAGNER: I'm your house guest.

CARSON: No, you're not.

RUTH: Oh, do let him. (*To* WAGNER) You could crawl under the bed. You'll feel at home there. I'll bet you're better under a bed than in it.

CARSON: Stop this.

WAGNER: Vouch for me, then. Lobby basis, I promise.

CARSON: What do you mean, lobby basis? This is the President of Kambawe, not some Downing Street P.R. man. Journalists here get hung up by their thumbs for getting his medals wrong.

WAGNER: Charming fellow, your boss.

CARSON: He's not my boss. He's the President, that's all. I can't help who's President. I'm a mining engineer.

WAGNER: They're his mines.

CARSON: They were here first and so was I. They're my bloody mines more than his.

RUTH: And more Shimbu's now than yours.

WAGNER: True.

CARSON: How did you know about all this?

WAGNER: I was guessing about Shimbu. On Mageeba I had my own source.

CARSON: No doubt—Canadian loudmouth.

WAGNER: Oh, yes.

CARSON: You know about the Canadians, do you?

WAGNER: Up to a point, Lord Copper.

CARSON: United Nations observers, they've been in Kamba City since Sunday.

WAGNER: And Shimbu's letter was to them, not to Mageeba . . . ? Just nod your head.

CARSON: I'll brief you if you promise to leave.

WAGNER: Sounds fair.

CARSON: Mageeba wants his mines back. Last year they produced nearly sixty percent of his copper—you read that in the *Kambawe Citizen*. The mines are no good to Shimbu because the railway goes the wrong way. You saw that on a map. So Shimbu will swap the mines for recognition of Adoma.

WAGNER: And he wants to talk through the UN people—the Canadians?

CARSON: Yes. To show good faith he says he won't fire a shot until he's fired upon.

WAGNER: Sounds sincere.

CARSON: Sounds as if he hasn't got all his armor up. Anyway, Mageeba bought it, he said he'd show up here with the Canadians at dawn, ready to talk. Halfway house, you see.

WAGNER: I'll believe the Canadians when I see them.

CARSON: Me too. Everybody's lying.

WAGNER: Tell me what you think.

CARSON: I think Shimbu wants the whole apple, and is using the time to get his supply line working. I think Mageeba isn't going to let Shimbu secede anywhere except into a ditch, and at breakfast time when he sees Shimbu hasn't fallen for it, he's going to go in with air strikes and tanks and lose half of them in a week, and appeal to the free world about Russian interference. I also think that the British and the Americans will protest, and all the time they're protesting the Russians will be interfering the stuffing out of Mageeba's army, until Kambawe is about as independent as Lithuania, and *that* the British and Americans will protest.

WAGNER: I see. I'll make sure the *Globe* puts that over.

CARSON: You'll what—?

WAGNER: I said I'll make sure the *Globe*—

But CARSON *is already laughing heartily.*

CARSON: Oh good! Oh wonderful! We're saved—the Prime Minister will be straight onto the Foreign Office—(*He mimes winding up an old-fashioned telephone while holding the ear piece.*) "Now look here, have you seen what those Russkies are up to in Africa?—the Queen is absolutely *furious* and so is Albert!"

WAGNER: All right.

RUTH: Poor Dick.

CARSON: Well . . . there you are.

WAGNER: Thanks, Geoff. (*Pours himself a drink.*)

CARSON: You said you'd leave.

WAGNER: I was lying.

CARSON: I'm beginning to wonder if you can be altogether trusted.

WAGNER: I'm sorry, but nobody on this story has got a sight of Mageeba since it broke. Let alone a quote. Let alone an interview. Let alone this deal with Shimbu. It's too big to pass up and I'm greedy for it—I admit that. I'm going to put the *Globe* so far out in front this Sunday, those roving correspondents and African specialists and bullshitters won't keep down their dinner for a week.

CARSON: Serve you right if he doesn't show up. He seldom does what he says.

But a car is becoming audible.

WAGNER: If he hadn't shown up I'd still be watching the compound. I saw him land fifteen minutes ago. Also two Sea King helicopters. Yeah. He's going to have Shimbu for breakfast all right.

The car is getting louder.

CARSON: Are you going?

WAGNER: No.

CARSON: Be careful if he laughs.

CARSON *goes out to meet the car.*

RUTH: You're shaking.

WAGNER: That's because I'm scared. What do I call him?

RUTH: He likes to be called "boy."

WAGNER: For Christ's sake.

RUTH: I'm beginning to like you a little.

WAGNER: Don't leave the room.

Then MAGEEBA *is in, followed by* CARSON, MAGEEBA *is in uniform, open-necked shirt, informal but well laundered and wearing medal-ribbon. He carries a short cane with a metal knob, and a toy machine gun with which he suddenly "sprays" the room.*

MAGEEBA: Mrs. Carson. A little present for your son. (*He presents the gun.*)

RUTH: Good evening, Your Excellency . . . how kind of you to honor us.

MAGEEBA: A pleasure . . . a beautiful home and a beautiful hostess. Please forgive this late hour.

RUTH: It's never too late—welcome . . . we're night birds here.

MAGEEBA: How gracious, . . . I, too, sleep very little.

RUTH (*gaily*): Well—uneasy lies the head that—

"RUTH" (*loudly*): Idiot!

RUTH: I mean the sheer volume of work must be enormous, the cares of States, and—

"RUTH": Shut up, you silly woman—

RUTH: May I introduce Mr. Richard Wagner?

MAGEEBA: Mr. Wagner.

WAGNER: Sir—your most—er—Excellency—

"RUTH": Compose yourself, Wagner.

MAGEEBA: You are a visitor to Kambawe?

WAGNER: Yes, sir.

CARSON: Would you care for anything, sir?

MAGEEBA: What brings you to Kambawe?

WAGNER: You do, sir—your determined stand against Russian imperialism in Africa has won the admiration of the British people—

"RUTH": Jesus Christ.

WAGNER: —sir, and I feel very privileged myself to have the opportunity to—

MAGEEBA *stops him with an upraised hand.*

MAGEEBA (*triumphantly*): Ah! (*To* CARSON) Your guest is a journalist.

CARSON: I'm very sorry about this, sir—Mr. Wagner arrived a few minutes ago quite by chance—he was just leaving—

RUTH: For London.

MAGEEBA: How I envy him. I have very happy memories of London. Student days, you know. I learned everything about economic theory. It has proved a great handicap. (*To* RUTH) How are things in London, Mrs. Carson?

RUTH: Oh—did you know I'd been?

MAGEEBA: My cousin tells me of all interesting and distinguished travelers.

RUTH: You have a cousin at the airport?

MAGEEBA: No, at the court of St. James.

"RUTH": Say goodnight, Gracie.

MAGEEBA: But I also have a cousin at the airport, of course.

RUTH: Oh good.

MAGEEBA: You see, I know everything. I am like a father to all citizens of Kambawe. In your case, of course, that would be difficult to imagine.

RUTH: Of course.

"RUTH": Wrong!

MAGEEBA: Such is our legacy of racial and cultural prejudice.

RUTH: Yes, indeed.

"RUTH" (*loudly*): Geoffrey!!

> WAGNER *decides to make his pitch and to do so quite formally. The effect is more wooden than formal.*

WAGNER: Your Excellency—Sir . . . I hope you will forgive my presence but as I say, the British people are watching with intense and sympathetic interest your courageous stand against the communist menace in Africa, and if you, sir, have any words of reassurance— however few—any message for the British people—and indeed the world—the *Sunday Globe* would be privileged to publish them.

> *Pause.* MAGEEBA *has been deciding on a chair and sinking himself into it. Now he looks up and looks at* WAGNER *apologetically.*

MAGEEBA: I'm so sorry, Mr. Wagner, were you speaking to me?

WAGNER (*bravely*): Yes, sir. I was saying, Your Excellency, that the British people are following with intense admiration and interest your . . . er . . . courageous stand against the communist threat in Africa . . . sir . . .

MAGEEBA: Yes?

WAGNER: Yes, sir, and if you have any message for the British people—and indeed the world—well, my paper would be privileged to publish it.

MAGEEBA (*pause*): The *Sunday Globe*.

WAGNER *nods*.

What a fascinating interview that was with Colonel Shimbu.

"RUTH": Run!

CARSON: Well, Dick, nice of you to drop in.

MAGEEBA: Is Mr. Wagner a friend of yours, Geoffrey?

CARSON: No—

RUTH (*simultaneously*): Oh, rather. We met in London. I'm terribly fond of him. (*To* WAGNER) I'll see you to the door.

WAGNER *finally, reluctantly, moves*.

MAGEEBA: Do you have to leave, Mr. Wagner?

WAGNER: Not at all.

MAGEEBA: Then you must stay.

"RUTH": You're bitched, Wagner.

MAGEEBA: I am interested to meet you. We must have a good talk. Sit down.

WAGNER: Thank you, sir.

MAGEEBA (*indicating a chair*): There.

CARSON (*worriedly*): Your Excellency . . .

MAGEEBA: Yes, you were saying, Geoffrey—a little whisky and water, then.

CARSON: Of course. Would you like the malt?

MAGEEBA: Not with water.

CARSON: No—of course.

MAGEEBA: The blended, about half and half, no ice.

CARSON: Whisky and water, no ice.

WAGNER: That will do me nicely, without the water.

WAGNER *is transformed, secure, pleased with himself.*

So I don't mind a bit of malt if you can spare it.

CARSON *uses* WAGNER's *bottle of Cutty Sark for the drinks.*

CARSON (*to* RUTH): Darling?

RUTH: Nothing.

CARSON: Ruth has arranged for a little late supper if you should care for something, sir.

"RUTH": He's not going to have room for a thing after Wagner.

MAGEEBA: Mr. . . . Wagner.

WAGNER: Mr. . . . President. Sir.

MAGEEBA: Mr. Wagner, it is not you, is it, who has to be congratulated on the *Sunday Globe*'s interview with Colonel Shimbu?

WAGNER: That wasn't me, sir, no. As a matter of fact, it wasn't a *Globe* reporter at all, it was a young freelance chap who found himself caught up with Shimbu quite by accident. Of course when he sent it to the *Globe*, they were bound to use it, because—well, all the news that's fit to print, as they say.

MAGEEBA: "The press lives by disclosure."

WAGNER: Ah, you know that one.

MAGEEBA: Delane of the *Times*—we had all that at the L.S.E. The political history of communications, or some such course.

He accepts his drink from CARSON.

Thank you. And C. P. Scott of the *Manchester Guardian,* of course—"Comment is free but facts are sacred."

WAGNER: Yes, and "Comment is free but facts are on expenses."

MAGEEBA: Scott?

WAGNER: Wagner. (*He takes his drink.*) Cheers.

MAGEEBA: What did you think of the Shimbu interview by the way?

WAGNER: Ah, well. (*He looks for safe ground.*) These chaps, they even talk like puppets, don't they? I think it's useful in a way to let them have their say. For that reason. Of course, sir, if you felt that some reply—or refutation—was indicated, I need hardly say that I, or rather the *Globe*—

MAGEEBA: You would give me equal space?

WAGNER: Oh—absolutely—

MAGEEBA: That's very fair. Isn't it, Geoffrey? Mr. Wagner says I can have equal space.

WAGNER: And some space is more equal than others. I think, Sir, I could more or less guarantee that an interview with you at this juncture of the war would be treated as the main news story of the day, and of course would be picked up by newspapers, and all the media, round the world.

MAGEEBA: What war, Mr. Wagner?

WAGNER: Sorry?

MAGEEBA: Kambawe is not at war. We have a devolution problem. I believe you have one, too.

WAGNER: A devolution problem? Yes . . . I see. Do you mind, sir, if I make a note or two?

MAGEEBA *waves permission and* WAGNER *takes a notebook from his pocket.*

MAGEEBA: If it is a war it is not of my waging. I am a man of peace . . . (*He waits for* WAGNER *and repeats as he writes*) man of peace. When a man strikes me without cause or warning, I invite him to breakfast. Don't I, Geoffrey?

CARSON: I have told Mr. Wagner that your visit is a social one, sir.

MAGEEBA: Quite right. I am going to have breakfast with Shimbu. At least—I have invited him to breakfast, I can do no more than that, and I don't mind at all, Mr. Wagner, that you are here to witness my good faith.

WAGNER: Absolutely.

"RUTH": Absolutely. Help.

WAGNER: Do you think Shimbu will come?

MAGEEBA: Yes. He might come early, perhaps, and bring his own food, but I think he would come. It would be to his advantage now to come to the breakfast table with a reasonable and peace-loving man. His methods have been piratical but his cause is not without interest. Our frontiers, you know, are still the frontiers of colonialism. Adoma has its own language, an ancient culture, and the people are of distinct appearance. This does not mean that Adoma could prosper as an independent nation—frankly it could not, except as the handmaiden of its so-called liberators, and I think Shimbu will see that there is more true independence in being, let us say, an autonomous state federated to Kambawe.

WAGNER: Are you offering that, sir?

MAGEEBA: I would consider a referendum. But of course that would depend on an immediate withdrawal from his present aggressive positions.

WAGNER: The Malakuangazi mines.

MAGEEBA: I don't think Geoffrey would accept anything less.

CARSON: He did rather come in without knocking.

MAGEEBA: And of course there is the question of uninvited foreigners. At this moment on Kambawe soil we have Russians, Cubans, Yemeni and Libyans. We even have a few Czech and German mechanics, I'm told. The American Ambassador asked me if I would let the United Nations come in. I said, half of them are already here—working for Shimbu.

WAGNER: Is there any UN presence in Kamba City yet?

MAGEEBA: No.

WAGNER: I see. And what if Shimbu doesn't come to the table and doesn't withdraw?

MAGEEBA: Then, Mr. Wagner, you may call it a war.

WAGNER: When may I do that, sir?

MAGEEBA: Would 10:00 A.M. suit you?

WAGNER *grins, drains his glass and holds it out to* CARSON.

WAGNER (*to* CARSON): May I . . . ?

"RUTH": On a packet of salt used in my grandmother's kitchen there was a label showing a girl holding a packet of salt with the label showing, and so on. It is said, with what authority I do not know, that this was the inspiration of Whistler's famous painting of my grandmother painting her self-portrait, the one he was painting. A different school holds that it was in fact the inspiration of Turner's painting of a packet of salt. During a storm at sea. Sorry. I was miles away. Come and sit down. I talk to myself in the middle of a conversation. In fact I talk to myself in the middle of an *imaginary* conversation, which is itself a refuge from some other conversation altogether, frequently imaginary. I hope you don't mind me telling you all this.

WAGNER: Do you have what you need to win the war?

MAGEEBA: If it's a short war.

WAGNER: And if it's not? Are you looking to us and the Americans?

MAGEEBA: I'd be a fool to do that. Your record of coward-
ice in Africa stretches from Angola to Eritrea.

CARSON: Lobby basis, Dick.

MAGEEBA: No—no—I don't believe in that. They asked me
if they could appoint a lobby correspondent in K.C. I
said, fine, tell him to go and sit in the Sheraton, it's the
most comfortable lobby in town. I know the British
press is very attached to the lobby system. It lets the
journalists and the politicians feel proud of their tradi-
tional freedoms while giving the reader as much of
the truth as they think is good for him. I have some
experience of the British press. When you granted us
our independence—as Geoffrey likes to refer to the
military victory of the Nationalist Front—the Kambawe paper was the property of an English gentleman. Isn't that so, Geoffrey?

CARSON: Well, not exactly, sir—

MAGEEBA: Not *exactly* a gentleman, no, but a rich
Englishman with a title. So there we were, an independent country, and the only English newspaper was
still part of a British Empire—a family empire—a chain
of newspapers—a fleet of newspapers, shall I say? Yes,
that's very good, not a chain but a fleet of newspapers.
That's good, isn't it, Mr. Wagner?

WAGNER: Yes . . . you mean like a convoy?

"RUTH": He means like Fleet Street, you fool.

MAGEEBA: Fleet Street—

WAGNER: Oh yes—very good—

MAGEEBA: Of course, we had many businesses controlled by overseas interests, we still have many, and we have many more partnerships—even the Kambawe Mining Corporation is such a partnership and you can see from that, can you not, Mr. Wagner, that we have no prejudice against English gentlemen as such—but a newspaper, a newspaper is not like a mine, or a bank, or an airline; it is the voice of the people and the Kambawe paper was the voice of an English millionaire.

WAGNER: Which one?

CARSON: Yours, Dick.

WAGNER: Oh . . . somewhat before my time, sir.

MAGEEBA: Nothing personal, Mr. Wagner.

WAGNER: Good God, I hold no brief for *him*.

MAGEEBA: I realize of course that you are only an able seaman on the flagship.

WAGNER: Well, sir, we've come a long way since we were galley slaves. Northcliffe could sack a man for wearing the wrong hat. Literally. There was a thing called the *Daily Mail* hat and he expected his reporters to wear it. Things are very different now.

MAGEEBA: Indeed, Mr. Wagner, now the hat your proprietor expects you to wear is metaphorical only.

WAGNER: With respect, sir, you underestimate the strength of the organized workers—the journalists—I'm with you on this one, if I may say so, sir—a newspaper is too important to be merely a rich man's property.

MAGEEBA: Yes. The power of the proprietor is too limited to do any good.

WAGNER: Too limited?

MAGEEBA: Naturally. A proprietor can only dismiss you from his *own* newspaper. The irresponsible journalist remains free to work elsewhere. No, I'm with *you* on this one, if I am to say so, Mr. Wagner. Collective responsibility. Let the journalists close ranks and be answerable to no one but themselves.

WAGNER *suspects he is being outflanked.*

WAGNER: Yes . . . well, they would be answerable to a democratically elected body representing the membership.

MAGEEBA: That's what I said. What do you think, Mrs. Carson?

RUTH *has relapsed into a "private" state, which may be indicated by lighting, but she is equal to the occasion.*

RUTH: I think I'll have that drink after all.

She goes to get it.

MAGEEBA (*to* RUTH): Yes, we should drink to Mr. Wagner's freedom.

RUTH: Is it in question?

She is momentarily concerned, but CARSON *explains . . .*

CARSON: His freedom to report.

RUTH: Ah, yes.

MAGEEBA (*raising his glass*): To the downfall of the English millionaires.

CARSON: I'm not sure that I ought to drink to that. I think I'm related to one or two.

MAGEEBA: Do they have newspapers?

CARSON: Oh, no, they're entirely respectable. (*To* WAGNER) Well, Dick, to freedom from millionaires—

RUTH: How strange. I had no idea that it was the millionaires who were threatening your freedom to report, Dick. *I* thought it was a millionaire who was picking up the *bill* for your freedom to report. In fact, I was discussing this very thing with somebody only yesterday—who could it have been?—oh, yes, it was Alastair . . . (*She smiles broadly at* WAGNER.)

WAGNER (*sarcastically*): Alastair, was it?

RUTH: "Allie," I said, "how *are* things in London with all those millionaires controlling the freedom to report?" "I don't quite follow you mummy," he said. "The whole country is littered with papers pushing every political line from Hitler to St. Francis." *His* theory— Alastair's theory—is that it's the very free-for-all which guarantees the freedom of each. "You see, mummy," he said, "you don't have to be a millionaire to contradict one. It isn't the millionaires who are going to stop you, it's the Wagners who don't trust the public to choose the marked card." Do you think he's got something, Dick?

WAGNER: I was talking about *national* papers.

RUTH (*eagerly*): That's *just* what I said to him. "Allie," I said, as I spread his Marmite, "it's absurd to equate the freedom of the millionaires to push *their* line with the freedom of a basement pamphleteer to challenge them." "Oh, mummy," he said, "don't be so *silly*. You are confusing freedom with capability. The *Flat Earth News* is *free* to sell a million copies. What it lacks is the capability of finding a million people with fourpence and the conviction that the earth is flat. You see, mummy," he said, "people don't buy rich men's papers because the men are rich: the men are rich because people buy their papers." Honestly, the things they teach them at Ascot Heath!

WAGNER: You pointed out, did you, that a man can be rich from oil or real estate and subsidize a paper on the profits?

RUTH: Of course. But he was ready for that one—apparently some of the chaps were thrashing it out in the boot-room after footer, and the general consensus of opinion in the Lower Third is that freedom is neutral. Free expression includes a state of affairs where *any* millionaire can have a national newspaper, if that's what it costs. A state of affairs, Allie says, where only a particular approved, licensed, and supervised non-millionaire can have a newspaper is called, for example, Russia.

MAGEEBA: Or, of course, Kambawe.

RUTH (*simultaneously*): Kambawe . . . ,

"RUTH": Geoffrey!

CARSON: I'm sorry, sir—I know Ruth didn't mean—

MAGEEBA (*placatingly*): Please!

RUTH: I *am* sorry—he's such a chatterbox, Allie . . .

MAGEEBA: Please . . . please don't concern yourself. I enjoy a free and open debate. It is a luxury which a man in my position can seldom afford. And I admit that by the highest ideals the *Daily Citizen* is open to criticism. At the time of independence it was undoubtedly free. It was free to select the news it thought fit to print, to make much of it, or little, and free to make room for more and more girls wearing less and less underwear. You may smile, but does freedom of the press mean freedom to choose its own standards? Mrs. Carson?

RUTH: What's the alternative?

MAGEEBA: That was the question. Easy enough to shut the paper down, as I would have been obliged to do had it not been *burned* down during the state of emergency which followed independence. But what to put in its place? The English millionaire folded his singed tents and stole away the insurance money, which didn't belong to him since I had nationalized the paper well before the fire was out. Never mind—the field was open. I did not believe a newspaper should be part of the apparatus of the state; we are not a totalitarian society. But neither could I afford a return to the whims of private enterprise. I had the immense and delicate task of restoring confidence in Kambawe. I could afford the naked women but not the naked scepticism, the carping and sniping and the public washing of dirty linen which represents freedom to an English editor. What then? A democratic committee of journalists?—a thorn bush for the editor to hide in.

No, no—freedom with responsibility, that was the elusive formula we pondered all those years ago at the L.S.E. And that is what I found. From the ashes there arose, by public subscription, a new *Daily Citizen*, responsible and relatively free. (*He leans toward* WAGNER.) Do you know what I mean by a relatively free press, Mr. Wagner?

WAGNER: Not exactly, sir, no.

MAGEEBA: I mean a free press which is edited by one of my relatives.

He throws back his head and laughs. WAGNER *joins in uncertainly.* RUTH *smiles nervously.* CARSON *looks scared.* MAGEEBA *brings the weighted end of his stick down on* WAGNER's *head.* WAGNER *falls on the floor.*

(*Shouting*) So it doesn't go crawling to uppity niggers!—so it doesn't let traitors shit on the front page!—so it doesn't go sucking up to liars and criminals! "Yes sir, Colonel Shimbu, tell us about the exploitation of your people!—free speech for all here, Colonel Shimbu, tell us about the wonderful world you're going to build in that vulture's garbage dump you want to call a country"—yes, you tell us before you get a machine gun up your backside and your brains coming down your nostrils!—who's going to interview you then, Colonel, sir!

MAGEEBA *has stood up and moved away from* WAGNER. WAGNER's *head is bleeding slightly above the hairline.*

(*Evenly*) I'll give him equal space. Six foot long and

six foot deep, just like any other traitor and communist jackal.

The jeep is heard arriving.

CARSON: Shimbu?

MAGEEBA *gestures to* CARSON *to let the visitor in; but
before* CARSON *reaches the door* GUTHRIE *enters.
He is somewhat the worse for wear. He glances
around the room and then ignores everybody and
walks diagonally right down stage to where* WAGNER
is. His words are only for WAGNER.

GUTHRIE: Dick. Jacob's dead.

CARSON (*in response to* MAGEEBA's *glance of en-
quiry*): This is Mr. Guthrie, Your Excellency, he is
also from—er—London.

GUTHRIE *crosses to* MAGEEBA *and stands close to him.*

GUTHRIE: Are you the President of this shit-house country?

WAGNER: George . . .

GUTHRIE: Is it you that runs that drunken duck-shoot
calls itself an army?

WAGNER *and* CARSON *are moving in on him.* WAGNER
grabs GUTHRIE *and starts pulling him away.*

(*Shouts*) I don't call that a fucking cease-fire! I hope
they blow their fucking heads off!

WAGNER *has got* GUTHRIE *back down into a chair, and
holds him down.* RUTH *comes forward.*

RUTH: Where's Jacob?

GUTHRIE: In the jeep.

RUTH: In the jeep? What's he doing there?

GUTHRIE *doesn't reply.* RUTH *starts to leave.*

GUTHRIE *(sharply)*: Don't turn nim over—he'll come away in your hand.

RUTH *moans and sinks down where she is.*

WAGNER: Jesus.

CARSON: I'm sorry. What happened?

GUTHRIE: We never got to Snimbu.

MAGEEBA: Your messenger, Geoffrey?

CARSON: Yes. *(To* GUTHRIE*)* Have you got the letter?

GUTHRIE: Jake had it. I suppose it's still in his bag.

CARSON *leaves the room, going to the jeep.*

(To WAGNER*)* You've got blood on your head.

MAGEEBA: Well, Mrs. Carson. I must say goodnight. Thank you for your gracious hospitality. *(To* WAGNER*)* I will remember what you said, Mr. Wagner.

WAGNER: What was that . . . sir?

MAGEEBA: Why, that my determined stand against communist imperialism is being watched with admiration by the British people.

WAGNER: Oh, yes.

MAGEEBA: Congratulations on your Mageeba interview. Oh—did you have any further questions?

WAGNER: No, I don't think so.

MAGEEBA: I shall look forward to reading the *Sunday Globe* this week. The main news story of the day I think you said. I take my hat off to you. I'm sorry if I was rude about yours. Oh, one more thing, Mr. Wagner—would you make a note . . . it was not Othello I played at Charterhouse. It was Caliban. They always get it wrong.

MAGEEBA *exits.*

GUTHRIE: He hit you? Because he didn't like your hat?

WAGNER: That's right.

GUTHRIE: These are the good guys. We get accredited by the good guys.

RUTH: So what happened to Jacob?

GUTHRIE: It was right outside Malakuangazi. Just getting dark.

MAGEEBA'S *car has been heard to leave.* CARSON *enters.*

It took us twice as long to get there as Geoffrey said. Mageeba's pass worked but it worked slowly. We eventually got to the front, which is where the cover runs out. You could see Malakuangazi across a strip of open land, no dead ground. We had the headlights on, acting friendly, and a white handkerchief tied to the aerial, but it was just about dark, they couldn't see what was coming. We got a couple of hundred yards, and they put up a flare. That was O.K. But somebody behind us got nervous and let off a few rounds. You know—shooting at a town with a rifle—that sort of discipline. So that gets somebody else excited, and pretty soon there's a cross-fire, and another flare, and we're the only moving object in sight. There's only one smart thing to do and Francis knows it. He stops the jeep and runs and I shouted to Jake to run and I got fifty yards and when I looked back he's in the driving seat trying to turn the jeep around. He got it around, and then he was hit. Knocked him into the back seat. I should have looked after him better. Stupid sod. Up till then he was having a good time.

WAGNER: You went back to the jeep?

GUTHRIE: I didn't know if he was dead. Engine was O.K. Only the windshield smashed. So I killed the lights and drove it back. But he was dead all right. A whole burst, head and shoulders. Heavy machine gun, I should think, just spraying around. He didn't know anything about it anyway.

CARSON: Where's Francis?

GUTHRIE: He ran the other way, toward Shimbu.

CARSON: Why?

GUTHRIE: I don't know. Maybe he knew something.

CARSON: My God. You were taking a hell of a chance, going in after dark.

GUTHRIE: We were already six hours behind.

CARSON: Shimbu was a long shot anyway.

GUTHRIE: Not Shimbu. The *Globe* is a Sunday paper. If you miss it by an hour you've missed it by a week. Story could be dead as a—I mean (*To* WAGNER) he wanted to go in, Dick. It wasn't just me.

WAGNER *nods.* CARSON *touches* RUTH's *shoulder.*

CARSON: I've got to follow Mageeba to K.C. There's nothing to worry about. He needs to talk to me about the mines, doesn't want to bomb the bits that matter. (*To* WAGNER) I'm taking the helicopter. I'll dump you two at the airport, but after that you're on your own. Get on any plane you can, and with luck you'll be out of the country before Mageeba has time to think about you.

WAGNER: No. I want to file from here.

CARSON: I'm already sticking my neck out for you. You've got time to get out and file.

WAGNER: No, I don't like that—planes can be late. Let me think.

GUTHRIE: You can file first from K.C. Get an AP wire. You have to risk that. And then a plane. Gives you two chances.

WAGNER: Yes, that's good. O.K. What about Jake?

CARSON: There's no proper morgue in Jeddu. I'll take the body to K.C. Do you know anything about his family? Who to tell?

WAGNER: Only the *Globe*. I'd better let them know *that* at least. All right?

CARSON: You can try.

> WAGNER *goes to the telex and switches it on, and taps some keys.*

We'll take the jeep down to the compound.

WAGNER (*over his shoulder to* GUTHRIE): Jeep picture?

> GUTHRIE *pats his camera bag.*

GUTHRIE: I shot some stuff before starting back. It was an artillery war when I left.

CARSON (*to* WAGNER): If you can't get straight through you'll have to leave it.

WAGNER: All my stuff's at the hotel.

CARSON: Forget it.

WAGNER: And the car?

CARSON: I'll get it picked up some time.

GUTHRIE: It's my car. I want it.

WAGNER *leaves the telex and comes back to* GUTHRIE.

WAGNER: What do you mean? Are you going back to Malakuangazi?

GUTHRIE: I thought I would, yes.

WAGNER: There's always other stories, Gigi.

GUTHRIE *is putting rolls of exposed film into linen envelopes which are prepared, labeled.*

GUTHRIE: I fancy this one. Here. Tell the AP man to print up that, I marked it—and wire anything which looks worthwhile. Tell him to push it to eight hundred and bugger the grain, I was using moonlight and flares. This one is for the London plane if you can get a pigeon.

CARSON: I don't think you understand. Mageeba is unpredictable. He may decide he was amused by your effrontery and give you a decoration, or he may feed you to the crocodiles. If I were you I wouldn't take the chance. He can always post you the decoration.

GUTHRIE: No, I don't think so.

CARSON: Look—first that Shimbu interview, and now you calling him names—he's not going to think the *Globe* is on his side.

GUTHRIE: We're not here to be on somebody's side, Geoffrey. That was World War Two. We try to show what happened, and what it was like. That's all we do, and sometimes people bitch about which side we're supposed to be on. (*To* WAGNER) Remember that Brass Hat in Saigon? "When are you guys going to get on the team?" *The team!* Give me the keys. I'll go by the hotel and get your stuff out.

WAGNER *hands over the car keys.*

WAGNER: Use my room. You should crash for a few hours.

GUTHRIE: No, I want to get back to Malakuangazi. It'll all be happening this morning.

WAGNER: I'll see you then. Take care, George.

CARSON: Good luck, George.

RUTH: I hope they blow your head off, George.

CARSON: Come on, Ruth.

RUTH: No, I won't. (*To* GUTHRIE) Tell me something, George. Which page is it on?

GUTHRIE: What?

The newspapers are still in the room and RUTH *picks up one of them.*

RUTH: This thing that's worth dying for.

GUTHRIE: I don't intend to die for anything.

RUTH: Jake did. (*With the paper*) Show me where it is. It can't be on the back page—(*reading*) "Rain Halts Australian Collapse." That's not it, is it? Or the women's page—(*reading*) "Sexy or Sexist?—The Case for Intimate Deodorants." Is that it, George? What about readers' letters—(*reading*) "Dear Sir, If the Prime Minister had to travel on the seven fifty-three from Bexhill every morning we'd soon have the railwaymen back on the lines." Am I getting warm, George?

WAGNER: You're belittling his death.

RUTH (*angrily*): You bet I am. I'm not going to let you think he died for free speech and the guttering candle of democracy—crap! You're all doing it to impress each other and be top dog the next time you're propping up a bar in Beirut or Bangkok, or Chancery Lane. Look at Dick and tell me I'm a liar. He's going to be a hero. The wires from London are going to burn up with congratulations. They'll be talking about Wagner's scoop for years, or anyway Wagner will. It's all bloody ego. And the winner isn't democracy, it's just business. As far as I'm concerned, Jake died for the product. He died for the women's page, and the crossword, and the racing results, and the heartbreak beauty queens and somewhere at the end of a long list I suppose he died for the leading article too, but it's never worth *that*—

She has started to swipe at GUTHRIE *with the newspaper and she ends up flinging it at him. Then she turns away.*

GUTHRIE: What's the name of the hotel?

WAGNER: I forget. Green awnings.

CARSON: The Sandringham.

WAGNER: Oh, yeah. I should have used that.

GUTHRIE (*approaching* RUTH): I've been around a lot of places. People do awful things to each other. But it's worse in places where everybody is kept in the dark. It really is. Information is light. Information, in itself, about anything, is light. That's all you can say, really.

(*He exits.*)

CARSON: Go to bed, darling. I'm sorry about having to go. I'll bring Allie back anyway.

RUTH: Will it be all right for him here?

CARSON: Oh yes. If it's not, I don't want you here either. I'll have some news before I leave K.C. (*To* WAGNER) Fit?

The telex has started chattering.

If that's London, make it quick. (*To* RUTH) Do we have an old blanket or something like that?

RUTH: Just take anything.

CARSON *goes out.* WAGNER *has gone to the chattering telex. It doesn't chatter for long.* WAGNER *stands reading the message as it comes off the machine. The machine stops.* WAGNER *continues to stare at it for a few moments. Then he turns away and goes to his Cutty Sark bottle and pours himself a drink and then takes the drink back to his chair and sits down.*

London?

WAGNER: Yes.

RUTH: Well?

WAGNER: There's no hurry.

CARSON *comes back with a ground sheet.*

CARSON: Allie's ground sheet. I'll get him another one. (*To* WAGNER) All right? What are you doing?

He's crossing to the telex.

Did you get it?

CARSON *tears the message out of the machine and looks at it. He comes back into the room with it.*

It's yours. From someone called Battersby. "Milne copy blacked by subs, full chapel and machine room support. Total confrontation and dismissal notices to-night, weekend shutdown definite. Wotwu—" Is that a garble?—"Wotwu—Battersby." What's that?

WAGNER: The *Globe* isn't printing this week.

Pause.

CARSON: What about your story . . . Oh. That's rotten luck, Dick.

He gives WAGNER *the telex message.*

WAGNER: Yeah. Wotwu.

CARSON: What is that?

WAGNER: Workers of the world unite.

CARSON: I see. What will you do now?

WAGNER: I'm just thinking. Would you air freight George's film for me? There's no rush.

CARSON *receives the envelopes from* WAGNER, *or just picks them up.*

CARSON: Yes, all right.

WAGNER: Telex the weigh-bill number to the office and they'll pick them up C.O.D. I'll call the hotel and get George to come back and fetch me. There may be a paper next week, and as he says, it'll all be happening this morning. I ought to be there.

RUTH: Aren't you supposed to be withdrawing your labor?

WAGNER (*snaps at her*): Don't get clever with me, damn you. (*Pause. To* CARSON) I'm sorry.

RUTH: That's all right.

CARSON: What about your story? Can't they do anything with it?

WAGNER: Yes, they could make paper airplanes with it. We'll see. Thanks for everything, Geoff.

CARSON: Drop by again.

WAGNER: I will.

CARSON (*to* RUTH): I'll phone fom K.C.

CARSON *leaves.* WAGNER *empties his glass and stands up.*

WAGNER: Could I have another drink?

RUTH: You brought it.

WAGNER *refills his glass and goes to the telex. He switches it on.*

RUTH: What are you doing?

WAGNER: Short piece about Jake. Onpass *Grimsby Messenger.*

RUTH: Good idea.

The jeep is heard leaving.

I think I'll have one too. Nightcap. No point in staying sober now he's gone, eh?

WAGNER: Jake?

RUTH: The President.

She takes his drink and puts it on top of the telex.

RUTH: Are you going to call George?

WAGNER: In a while. He won't be there yet. Did you have a thing for Jake?

RUTH: No.

WAGNER *is working the keyboard, pausing for thought. He stops to loosen his tie and light a cigarette.*

RUTH: Well, it was a very elevated, intellectual sort of thing. I wanted to undress him with my teeth. Oh God, I'm tired as hell and I'm not going to get to sleep.

WAGNER: Don't you have a pill for that?

RUTH: There *are* no pills for that. I want to be hammered out, disjointed, folded up and put away like linen in a drawer.

K19

She goes back to the whisky bottle and holds it upside down over her glass, and examines the label.

You can use the phone upstairs if you like.

WAGNER: I thought you didn't want to be a tart . . .

RUTH: How do I know until I've tried it? I name this bottle "Cutty Sark."

She breaks the bottle against the marble shelf and drops the remainder into the bin. She looks back at WAGNER: *he's at the keyboard, tie loose, cigarette in mouth, whisky on the "piano lid." It looks like a familiar piano-player-plus-singer scene. We hear the piano. Something fast.* RUTH *sings. Just a few bars. ("Lady is a Tramp")*

"RUTH" (*singing*): She gets too hungry for dinner at eight, Loves the theater but never comes late, She doesn't bother with people she hates—that's why the lady is a—

WAGNER *disrupts this by tearing the paper out of the machine. He comes and stands next to her.*

RUTH: Is that it?

WAGNER: That's it.

Blackout.